THE WAY
WE ARE

ROBERT PAUL GWYNNE

BALBOA.
PRESS
A DIVISION OF HAY HOUSE

Balboa Press books may be ordered through booksellers or by contacting:

Balboa Press
A Division of Hay House
1663 Liberty Drive
Bloomington, IN 47403
www.balboapress.com.au
1 (877) 407-4847

Print information available on the last page.

ISBN: 978-1-5043-1534-0 (sc)
ISBN: 978-1-5043-1535-7 (e)

Balboa Press rev. date: 02/11/2019

CONTENTS

Introduction

I have a belief, that is, a personal belief in myself, with regard to my being alive in this world of ours, that I am on a journey. I am yet to understand, to really and fully understand the reason for this life journey.

I am (in the following pages) talking about my own, and maybe, or possibly, your personal life journey. KNOW, that I totally respect each person's personal way of living, or you could say, "BEING ALIVE."

Thinking always, I am a minute part of the human race, "That I am alive, and am I getting my job done."

Living in harmony with my thoughts and feelings, maintaining such as thy are to me, MY own very personal inner sense of total integrity and honesty, or, just plain being alive.

BUT!

Why am I here, why did I choose Australia, my parents, my two brothers, my various vocations?

Why am I healthy and content with my life, and personal beliefs?

One day, I might find out, and if I don't? SO, BE IT.

What I may mention, in the pages following also applies to me, the person writing this.

This book was not intended to be lengthy. It was intended to be a short document on living and life.

We shall see!

But, as we live our lives, it certainly does not appear to me, and more certainly, most of us, that our lives and living as we do, is not unimportant.

Why do we make our lives and living experiences so complicated?

Or do we!

Is it possible, that life, our human life in this world of ours is, or could be, really simple?

Do we as humanity, inevitably set about making things complicated or difficult?

Where has simplicity, as we might think of the past, disappeared to? OR has it really!

Is humanity developing (whatever developing may mean to you!) at a pace that will inevitably leave some people behind?

Is it necessary to keep up to date on the path humanity appears to be on, specifically with regard to current & future technological advancements and modalities?

Am I referring to technology, and the telephone too, that is now computer driven, and their probability to assist in the creation of a different world?

Or, as I create this document, the IPad or whatever else is around, such as computer driven televisions, telephones, or, what next?

Why in the previous question do I use the word "different" rather than "better"?

That might then raise the question,

"Are we different from or are we better (or maybe worse), than previous generations."

And what of one of the current scourges bedeviling humanity?

The scourge of depression which affects one in five persons in the community.

So many questions!

Maybe, not so many or too few answers!

As might be stated in older or previous generations:

"ON WITH THE MOTLEY!"

A Starting Point or Two

As you commence reading these words I would like you to know that they were written, by someone who considers himself to be an ordinary person.

I am male, and for the girls who are reading these first lines, I have it on good authority and opinion, that ordinary males just don't exist.

Maybe, we can discuss this one later!

So, who am I? Why do I consider myself ordinary?

Just as importantly, what is my story?

Not like questions, but as comments that may or might, require an answer of some sort.

It is generally acknowledged that males tend to be more left brained and practical as distinct from the females, who are more right brained and intuitive.

Now, there are possibly or likely to be some of you, who are assessing or preparing for a discussion on this overall and not very correct point of view.

So, I would ask you to be a little tolerant of my giving this maybe, or possibly incorrect statement.

BUT, for me, the mention of right brained intuition is totally relevant.

As a male of our species, I was (as a youngster of about 10 years of age) instructed by a well-meaning uncle to be the man of the family.

My father had just died, and my mother had arranged I visit an uncle, a master craftsman in woodworking, who previously had given me instruction in that trade.

I remember vaguely, the reason for the discussion, and why it had to take place.

In those long-ago days, left and right brain applications to life were rarely or never mentioned.

This was a left brained instruction if ever there was one.

It was basically – "be successful in life and look after your mother"

And, I took it on without further thought, as regards to the how, and/or why.

Until a few years ago, recently I suppose, I lived my life knowing I had no option, but to make positive, workable and very "no option", correct or right brain decisions.

At this point, in my life, I make no apologies to anyone for my pro-active ability to make decisions, and act in accordance with those decisions.

This personal attitude to life and living, is one reason for my professional success. But, at the same time, I am totally aware that this way of being has its own shortcomings.

Put this in another way, there is an ultimate personal payoff. BUT - As this writing has other things to talk about, the payoff is, and has become, a very personal attribute.

In that, on a personal level, those who know me, consider my shortcomings tolerable,

And come to me, as a friend, for a way of assisting their resolution problem.

There is another part of me, that does not believe he has done anything extraordinary in his life, and yet knows this is not a real truth, if it were viewed from all the perspectives of family members, personal friends, fellow students and professional clients.

Specifically, referencing my professional career over many, many years, clients and friends have achieved successes, way beyond their initial expectations.

You may ask: "Where do these people come in as part of the scene?"

As a professional Public Accountant, and CPA of very many years, an occult student for some fewer years, a Reiki Practitioner, friend to others, a father to three, and step-father to another three, I acknowledge and know and appreciate, that people play a very important part in my life.

I am not specifically referring to financial success, but something like a very personal, we might say outrageous, life and living success, that at the start, seemed to be an impossible dream.

Dear reader, there are many stories that make up the contents of the previous paragraphs.

I request again, your indulgences.

Keep reading, I am certain that in one, or maybe all of the following chapters, you will find answers. Answers that can or will, somewhat fit.

YOUR personal perspective on YOUR life, and LIVING, and WAY OF BEING.

Thus, for me, all things are an important part of this My Story.

Each and every person we meet in our lives, will (regardless of our allowing it or not), have an impact on who and what we are, as we live, and as we as individuals, impact on those who choose to keep our company.

At some point in our lives, maybe as younger people, maybe as we grow older, or maybe at an appropriate, or inappropriate and suitably reflective mood; "WE GET IT"!
We get, what in this day and age could be termed a "LIGHT BULB MOMENT".

For me, a particular "thought" or more like a realisation, occurred some 20 years ago, which at the time certainly did not appear to me as anything important, but more like "I Wonder".

Please bear with me as I work through what is to my mind, important stuff from the past and subsequent occurrences.
Before I define "the thought" in greater detail. The unfolding of that "thought" has its own importance.
It also had, and still has, wider implications than "the thought" itself.
As I was to discover over time.

I have referred to that point in time, to many people as an acknowledgement.

To me, at the time, it was only a point of observation.

When it happened, it was somewhat meaningless.

My left brained activity dropped the essence of the "thought" because the thought had no practical use.

Let's face it! Life works! You get on with what you have to do, as part of your daily activities, or your working life, and/or your family life.

There is mostly little, of importance, that will immediately change the current circumstances of your life, and the way you are presently living it.

Home is home, work is work, pleasure is pleasure, and enjoyment is enjoyment – siblings are children - and so on.

But is this correct?

In the way we might, or could live our lives if something were to change, or?

Is it possible that the above, and many other daily living things, such as your children, housework, entertainment, sleep, travel, and so on, could be part of our very personal each other, and at the same time, be part of something else?

If we have a partner to share these things with, they too become part of a second by second existence, and/or so do our friends, close or otherwise, our workmates, our sporting team, and others who see us, and as we see them, from their own particular perspective.

All become part of and are an extension of our second by second personal meaningful existence.

THE THOUGHT PROCESS

For most of us, regardless of where we're at, or what we're
doing, the thought process is part of our life and living
At an unlikely moment in time "THE THOUGHT" occurs.

I am not referring to a thought of something that should be
done, a thought of something to do later on that day, or in the
future or even maybe something that might have been done
sometime in the past.
That kind of thought is I believe, how we all live our lives.

I am talking of a thought that has nothing to do with what is
going on, or what might eventuate at the moment the thought
comes into existence.
Remember always, that the thought took less than a second
to come into existence and depart somewhere else.
Except that the "guts" of that instant fleeting thought stays in
your mind, complete - very complete.
In the instant it occurred, it remains.
Or, it is there, having its own, complete and separate type of
existence.

The subsequent effort to make a change, because of that one
single thought, to move out of an existing comfort zone where
we were at that thought moment!
Most times, is not possible.
The thought will still have no reason for its existence, it came
from nowhere, but it will be, and is, retained by your memory.
It can be perceived. It exists and is there.
And is most often, regarded by most of us, as an unsafe way
to live our lives.

The mingling of our created, daily living items and requirements, is the current creation of our present personal world - such as it is.

Change for change's sake is not an option, for or to, most of us. And, most times, we all tend to believe, any change is not an option.

Also, people might wonder as to the why, and can become suspicious about just what is going on or happening to; someone who unexpectedly appears to have changed, or is changing course.

Life and living, continues.

Each of our personal actions defines where we are, and who we are, on that second by second existence that makes up our meaningful day.

We all, from time to time, come across what could be called "New Age Ideas" or of "Life Changing" modalities.

I must stress, that I am in no way going to imply that the various methods of self- improvement as promoted by those various organisations should be ignored.

Similarly, there are various religious, and philanthropic organisations, and new age churches promoting life activity learning.

Each of these organisations or religious philosophies, may have something to offer you!

All these approaches to life and living have much to offer each and every one of us.

That is, if we wish to take part, knowing there is something to learn, and we have the time, energy and money.

On a personal level, one activity I took part in, has had a lasting effect on my perspective on life and living.
But then again other activities at their completion have left me enthused and ready for new things.
Looking back, I find that I do not remember any of these "change your life" activities as such. Maybe they did, and maybe they didn't, make a difference in my ultimate way of "being" as a human.
I believe, all of us are aware, that for most of us, our lessons in life are our way of living, and nothing is going to change our ultimate perspective on this.

Do not think for a moment, that I am impertinent enough to suggest your life and its daily pattern have the possibility of being meaningless and unimportant.
There are so many of you out there, who do live meaningful lives, not only for your families and friends, but for your community, and maybe the world in general.

You are, and you are: - "OKAY, THE WAY YOU ARE."
There is no obligation or reason to change or be different from who you are at this time, or ever for that matter.
Especially, if you know and believe you are content and happy, with the way things are.

Even so, I sometimes wonder what I am about, in my day to day travels through life and living.

There are days when from a very personal observation I appear to achieve little, and other days when lots seems to get done.

In the evening, I might hear on TV a report of a person, who in my opinion has done remarkable things, someone who has what appears to be a very full life of assisting others, someone in their community, or in a third world country.

Do the activities of these wonderful givers of time and energy, make me a lesser person?

I could answer yes, those actions can.

But only, if I, personally decide, in my own mind, that this is to be!

Thus, with reference to any other person by way of conversation of any sort, I am not able and ultimately will not change my personal thought pattern to be someone or something different.

Deep down, you know you could do the remarkable things you read and hear about.

Is it appropriate, for you and yours, your friends and acquaintances, partners and others to whom you relate, to do these things or something that is to you equally more important?

Possibly yes! Maybe no!

If any thought is to be acted on, we will Always consider the possibility that we are comfortable in our present daily living, existence and way of being.

So, we might sometimes wonder what we could do---.

To create some sort of change in our community and what might be the resultant implications.

We might just go out and deliberately do something different, just to make a difference somewhere or somehow.

We might possibly assist in a community activity, just for the sake of seeing what might happen.

I know of a number of people who have considered the possibility of becoming councillors for their local council. Ignoring the cost of undertaking this venture, some serious thought may have taken place.

Of all the conversations with many, over the years, only one younger person actually went out and became a councillor.

He was disappointed at restrictions which did not allow him, or that council, to undertake ALL the things he considered important for his community.

For each of us, certainly as we become older, the thought comes and is then considered: "Will one really, in the long term, make a difference?"

Does this become: "A difference to what, and/or, a difference to whom?"

Our present existence, in this personal world of ours, is the result of our past actions and activities.

If you were to find in the long term, nothing has changed, a reflective thought will confirm you are doing things the way you always did.

So, BE COMFORTABLE.

The change thought, might not be appropriate or worthy of any effort, on reflection.

It is important to understand that; as you read this, you are complete.

There is nothing wrong, bad, good, right, that is possibly remotely appropriate to change you from the persona that makes up your current existence, your life and your way of living.

There are some of you who will say to yourselves as you read the last paragraph, "But what about the thieves, arsonists, con-men (and women) and so on?"
Do you view (as you read the previous statement) their existence from your own personal moral perspective?
Is it possible that they, from their own personal perspective consider their lives complete?

We all know, maybe only in a subtle way, that we are loved or liked for who and what we are by our family, friends and acquaintances.
And, there are others we come into contact with, who will never be a part of our lives.

There are those of you, who have in the past, attempted to become someone different, maybe for the sake of a perceived special relationship, and have discovered that in being someone else, or someone you really are not, you are being untrue to your real self, or your subtle, mental, vital self: "Your true personality".
Thus, we either become confused, or the untrue relationship based on untrue actions abruptly ceases.

Sitting alongside this is the knowledge that some relationships, that were regarded as being "for life" at the time, no longer exist.

Each of us has moved on in some way, to another place.

Not like a distance, but as "a way of being" that we, or our friends, or family, find has no enduring interest.

Do not mourn these transient relationships.

They are/were important at the time they existed.

Know also, that you and they had the opportunity to learn something from each other at the time.

This is a subtle thing, the existence of which has become part of the person you now are, and possibly always were, from a very early age.

Each and every one of us lives our present life, out of our past experiences.

What we are at this point in time, is a result of our activities undertaken from birth to the present.

Do not mourn ignored opportunities, or those things not done, that might have made a difference in your own or someone else's life.

The past is the past and cannot be changed.

We always, on a continuing basis, have the opportunity to look to the future, if that is our wish.

And to go back to where I started, this might be where that "thought" dropped in. And we repeat the conversation of the previous pages over and over again.

I repeat what I have previously stated.

You are OKAY as you are.

There is no need to make changes in your life for the sake of change.

People associate with, and love you, as you are, and associate with you also because you are who you are.

They are comfortable with predictable you, and you, as you are reading this, will intuitively realise your life is working out as it has been designed by yourself.

All is well in your world!

Your world is as you have designed it!

I hear some of you saying, "All is not well in my world."

I repeat: "Your world is as you have designed it!"

There is always that, "what if, thought that exists" in the human thought process that continues to drop into our lives. Thought and thinking will continue, to come about as we work through our daily living existence.

Thoughts are ignored, or considered and acted on, or are put to one side as something to maybe do in the future – and this includes "THAT THOUGHT"

Know that all is well, and as it should be with you.

This is, "YOUR WORLD", your world of existence.

Your world, the one you have created.

Your world, the one you are continuously recreating.

If these previous words do not sit well with you, I ask you to read on.

You have got this far.

You will not be fair to yourself, let alone those you love, respect, and those who associate with you, with love and respect, if you were to put this book down now.

There is so much that might be explained as I compose these document pages.

Life and our existence is about our own personal creativity, and the knowing of, and acceptance of, the fact that we are all capable and loved individuals.

With or without our very personal realisation(s), we create and keep recreating ourselves and, our present living environmental world around us, our physical existence.

WE do this on a daily continual basis.

And those thoughts, or "that thought", continue to drop in.

We can and do watch how others in our world create and recreate their world.

The others in this or their world, could be children, adults, even our own or other's pets, or the plants and flowers we co-exist with.

The whole of our existence, our place in the world, determines the who and the what of, and just who we are
Our life, in this world in which we live and exist.

Be at peace with yourself.
Know this is possible by "just being."
By being: "Just who you are."
By thinking: "The very personal way you have always done."
By allowing: "Personal thoughts to come and go."

And always, being just the same, in continuing to live your current life in exactly the same way you have always done!

May I now ask you to read on.

Look at some particular perspective that occurs often, in your daily living experience.
Know that they are not in any particular order or preference.

The chapters following are topics.

Just topics, that may or may not appeal to you at this moment in time.
And, if at some time, I do trust they may have some input for you to consider.
If not now – maybe or possibly at some time in the future.

How Do We Show Up In Life

I am reminded of a saying I heard many, many years ago.
It goes something like:
"You are OK the way you are! It takes lots of effort to change and be better".

Now, as a diversion from what is to come in this whole document; an important reflection on common usage of everyday words.
In this case, I am referring to the word "BETTER"

Better than WHO!
Better than WHAT!
Better than Who You ARE!
Or perhaps something like "BETTER THAN"?

There is another word that makes me cringe when it is used – and used far to often, and that word is "TRY"
In my opinion, if we are setting out to TRY something, we are setting out to fail!

When, the purpose of an approach to venture into something new is envisaged, the INTENTION of that activity is to succeed.
Surely not, to have it fail.

OR:

In common usage – humanity sets out to try something to see if it works, a complete waste of time and energy.

In your mind, on starting something, "KNOW" on a mental level you will be successful.

AND

At the same time, "KNOW" on that same physical level, it may take a few different ideas and applications to achieve the desired result, or maybe results.

Keeping in mind the first words of this, shall we say chapter, there is another adage that again comes to mind, one I recall from that same time period:

"You are OK the way you are".

This statement was given to me in my early years of learning to play the violin, as an eight-year-old.

"Believe; and know you will be successful in the years ahead"

As an aside, I joined the Australian Navy (Band Branch) at age 15, as a Boy Musician and violinist, (had to learn to play a clarinet as a parade instrument too), almost on my arrival with my violin, had it placed under my chin with the word "PLAY". I got the immediate nickname "maestro", that day, from the other boys, my age and a little older. I knew I was good, but, not that good!

But, in the eyes of the other lads, learning to play a difficult string instrument, it was, in their eyes, a living truth.

No, it did not go to my head, but it gave me the opportunity to help others, the opportunity to be as good as myself, and be a member of the band, outside of the requirement to learn to march effectively, play my clarinet at the same time, and most importantly, be one of the boys.

Did I have any appreciation of what I was letting, or getting, myself into. "NO"

Do I know I was "eventually" successful, "YES".

The story of what eventuated in those intervening years is not for here, but is given as a small evidence piece of my personal learning, to validate in a fashion

The "believe" ending to the previous paragraph.

This was about not changing your beliefs, but paying attention to the believer.

I remember, at the time, thinking that the word "believer" meant something about oneself. A reference to me, as being the believer.

But more importantly, a realization of a total belief in myself – warts and all.

Some twenty years ago I attended a course run by the Werner Erhard organization, called "The Forum" now called by some other name, (maybe) if it still exists.

This very intensive four-day, (and 14 hours each day) seminar, was based on the statement, "What is the being of Human Being".

Its meaning: "Being" - The way we show up to others we know and meet maybe for the first, or other additional times.

As individuals, and, in an individual sort of independent way, which means that each of us, as we meet and greet previous or new people, is done in a certain personal way, by oneself, and/or the other person or persons.

Thus initially; the other person(s), is/are, prepared to cope with us (me)as an individual(s) exactly as THEY see or experience us.

I will not attempt to cover the complexity of those four days; however, I did clearly get to see in a very honest, personal way, how I actually do show up to my family, friends, clients, and others on a daily basis.

That, those other people, continue to allow me any form of relationship with them, is in its own way a contribution to me, rather than the other way around.
At the same time, I am able to contribute to these persons, (and especially my professional clients), in a more practical and rewarding way.

Within these words, I may in some way, be repeating myself. I request your tolerance if I do, in my efforts to pursue any particular or personally relevant line of thought.

So, for a moment let us go back to somewhere at the beginning. The "thought", came and went so fast.
That "thought" that had no meaning at the time.
And; there is more to come still, on that "thought".

For me, at this particular place in the narrative, there is no quick way to get to the end of the story.

I truly believe, we all work our way forward, in some personal fashion, to achieve a workable, creditable way of life.

If you don't realize this aspect of life and living, may I suggest you read the first few lines of the start of this chapter again.

Apart from all this, there is more to come on that "thought".

I have developed a practical, demanding personality, I have lived my life by making decisions, and making these decisions work, regardless of any opposition.
The left brained part of me was totally, and is mostly, still in control.

Statements in the past, and currently, now I am older, (to some small extent), have been made to me like; we tried this, it didn't work, you are not old enough, grow up, it can't be done, no one has done this before, get real, etc. etc.
Those statements, and similar comments were, as they are to this day, for me a challenge to be "right", and achieve a successful conclusion, regardless.

I have known for a long time that there is a cost to be this way. As long as I believe my life works for me, and from my perspective it does, then I am happy to have that cost. I am thus, basically content.

"What is the cost?" you might ask;
AND
"For every action there is a reaction."

To explain:
When I was born, girls were nurtured to be intuitive. Intuition was, and still is, in lots of respects a female right brained way

of being. Women tend to think in a lateral way, by thinking past the obvious.

Boys were born to be practical, work based, methodical, left brained children.

Our future ability to be the breadwinner was assured, as and when we left school.

That well-meaning uncle who, at the time of my father's burial, told me at the tender age of 10, "I had now to be the man of the house and look after my mother", made a very correct statement. Someone had to look after mum.

My 10 year old brain took the instruction very seriously. I had no option but to be right, to always make very correct decisions.

I have proved without a doubt (to me) that my life works because I have no option but to be the original "Mr. Right".

Yes - there was no option. And yet there was!

In this my present much, much older life, I have many times proved that this is, the way it is.

There is a cost to this personality trait.

People are wary of contributing to me, because my way is always better than anyone else's.

But, at the same time, it served me well in my professional business career.

Do not take the previous male, female aspects of humanity as any more than words, in mine or any (to me) literal sense. Know that there are always exceptions to any and every rule and generalisation.

I do, however, base some actions and words on activities I have noted with many people, over many years, and over many discussions and observations. I also would be right in saying that we all know someone who doesn't fit the pattern or mould (male or female) I have just presented.

Too often as we read what might be termed "self improvement books" we are requested, tempted, think about, or consider, that there is something different we could or should do in our lives.

This might mean we should or maybe could contemplate the consequences of our day to day lives and living.

We are often told (always by others) that some sort of personal change is appropriate and necessary.
We undertake the subtle things that are implied, and ultimately find we are still the same person we always were.
The ideas were good, they appealed to us and our personality. Maybe you are or were someone who knew what they were going to do to improve their lot in life, or maybe it seemed to be important to implement certain concepts or ideas.

The concepts were and are still valid, as a way of being, or maybe as someone in control of their lives.
There are others with whom I have maintained contact, where the same activity has had no lasting effect. Some of these people have gone on to experience other things, as they will tell it, to further their search for knowledge.

I sincerely believe this book is intended to be a continuing reference source for the reader.

It is not written to make you "better", because I have always explained to those that know me, "being better" is in reality "being different".

As stated much earlier, "Better" is a word much misused, because to be better, in the context of this missive, is in reality, to be different.

Ultimately, are we really being better, or are we being different?

In most instances no, as we are in the long term, still the person we always were.

We are comfortable with who we are, what we are, how we appear to others we know, and others we relate to in our daily lives.

We may not like this form of comfort we have created for ourselves.

Ultimately we do nothing tangible or lasting to change our own particular comfort zone, which has become our way of living, and being.

The word better, implies some sort of change.

On a personal basis, this would appear to each and every one of us as something that has, or might, in the future take place.

This is when there is an action undertaken to make your work, sport, life, living, more understandable, enjoyable or worthwhile.

I am not referring here to the feelings of health and wellbeing where one might feel better.

The concept here is the operative word of "feeling"; which is a very personal sense, and thus will become totally inexplicable, in its very personal concept and context to other people.

We often use this same word (better), to define our position as regards our day to day living.

We all tend to use phrases such as "I did it better."
Did you really do it "better" or did you do it in a different way.
Did this give you the feeling of improvement which felt like it was better?
I believe so!

As we progress through our daily lives we attempt different things on a basis that is important to us, as and when we complete our daily chores.

That "thought" drops in and we try something a little different, and we might feel better for the successful result.
"Better", thus becomes a feeling, as it should be, a feeling towards oneself that in most cases defies a true and full explanation.
That sense of feeling is personal.
It cannot be truly communicated to someone else.

In the explanation of what we claim we did better, we are really explaining that what we did, was different.
The feeling of better is no more than that, a personal feeling only present to our own, very personal sense of identity.

Those who listen to our explanations may feel in themselves a sense of something like "This could be better", but if you

and they were to openly discuss the feeling of "better" you would end up with totally different points of view, given your personal feelings, and or personal achievable results.
"Better, for you, is not necessarily "Better" to anyone else.

There are those of us who are always looking for ways of doing things "better" or "different(differently)".

We all know of those people who believe they always do things better than anyone else. They promote to us their better way. Keep in mind that they are really describing their way, of doing something differently.
In most cases we listen politely to their explanation(s) of how it was better for them, and how it would be better for us.
Then, almost always, we eventually dismiss the idea, concept or explanation as being unworkable or useless for ourselves.
Keep in mind at all times that where these instances occur, that someone might see us as someone needing help to be better.
This more often than not, could be a subtle or polite way of presenting to you a statement to do things differently.

Something else to think about, as regards being "Better"
AND YET-------------:
How often has the thought occurred to you that it might be a good idea to be like someone else you know?
Would or might it make you better?

To sort of explain:
A particular friend or family member might seem to have many friends.
They might seem to be on top of things.

Their life from your perspective, might seem that everything is working for them.

So much else in their lives might seem to be in existence, things that might seem to defy any explanation you could give.

We think; "It would be great to be the same or like them."

And we instinctively know that this is never going to happen.

Is it possible they might admire you, and your way of life and living?

Your acceptance of things, as the way they are, and so much else?

It takes a brave person to venture down the conversational path of the why, with that friend or family member, to discuss their very personal inner life expectations.

As human beings, we acknowledge our friends and family members.

For they, and we too, are the human beings they/we are, exactly for that reason and for no other.

We may not personally accept their personality traits or values in life. They are not us, but then, in the same instant of time, we know this.

We are all individuals.

We are all, all the time, on our own individual life path.

Do we really know on that particular day exactly who we are?

Do we have a valid view on any particular day, or day to day basis, of how we know and find them?

And, why should we do so anyway?

We all have friends and family members who admire us for some particular reason we just don't discuss.

I am referring here to the person who might not be the type of individual with whom we would normally associate.

They call or ring us to communicate their own day to day living experiences and we are tolerant of their side of the conversation.

Their ability to communicate to us is possibly important to them, and we do wonder why, but remain patient, as well as tolerant.

Do they, have the thoughts; "It would be great to be the same or like them?" How would we know?

There is usually no way we might pursue that particular question, even in any ordinary conversation, even if that conversation is a little one-sided because they wish to talk, certainly not listen.

Are we the one on the pedestal to be admired by someone else, and we didn't even know it?

And it may be unnecessary to know this.

Do we appear to others to be in charge of our lives?

Are we appearing to others to be complete and knowing?

Whatever might be the answer to these and possibly any other questions of the same ilk, it is not polite (except under very particular conditions) which are not for discussion here, to raise the subject.

Why is this so?

Is it because each of us usually has the view of that other person - as being fairly complete, warts and all.

And at the same time, we are all, each and every one of us, totally aware that nobody is perfect.

We can, as human beings, be very tolerant of other people's failings and aberrations, especially if we regard them as friends.

Not forgetting that some family members are more like friends than family. After all, this is the true warts and all personality of that friend who is likely to stand by us, as we would stand by them when the "chips are down".

Each of us would love, on occasion, to move out of our comfort zone, and be different.

To be different might mean to do something "better" (that word again), but will it be the end result to make us feel better, or different?

I think not.

We all live in our particular comfort zone of life and living, that which we have been developing over many a year.

Our personal successes, and failures in life, as we've grown up, and grown older, are a very personal result of our learning processes.

We know, trust and understand beyond anything else, that life works for us, in the concept of how we live and run our lives.

When we've decided to take on a partner, husband or wife, or have children, we have made a very deliberate decision to make some sort of change.
For some of us this change is viable and works. It doesn't make anything "better".
Just different.

But I wonder if, beyond the "commitment thinking process" we really, truly know or appreciate the responsibilities we are taking on?
Looking back on my first marriage, I thought I did at the time, especially with regard to children.
But: eventually for me, it didn't work out the way – (in my mind) I had intended.

Pertinent for me to mention here, I have absolutely no regrets. I will, in a later chapter, cover why I think this way.

Some of us find the attempt at change doesn't work and the relationship concludes.

That it does not always conclude amicably is not for discussion here.

Did the relationship end because at some point we were making a change for a reason other than that which would be regarded by our personal inner selves as being totally true?

Often, we attempt to emulate someone or something, where at a particular point in time we have thought, could there be a better (different) way

As explained before, change for change's sake in an individual person's persona does not necessarily change the way a person appears, or thinks, as regards the existing friendship or relationship.

As you read this, you may have come to the realization that I am not using the word "thought" in the context of the explanation process. The human personal thought process continues to exist as an almost moment to moment activity. To avoid thinking and have thoughts is to avoid being alive. Thought, and thinking, are a daily living processes, very essential to our being alive, and, having the ability to make decisions.

How we appear to others in life is the result of our past, present and future thought and thinking processes.

There are, certain religious sects that have forms of meditation.
Ways of being that can, mostly with practice, still the mind from unwanted thoughts.
This may suit those people who might be regarded as adepts, and who are attempting to attain some ultimate (possibly religious) goal in life, but for most of us, this is not an option.

Day to day living demands continual thought about the past, what to do now, next, or what is necessary for us now, and into the future.
Thought that occurs in an almost automatic fashion.
At the same time there are periods where we all wish to have the opportunity to retire from the continual necessity for

thought. That rare opportunity, to retire into, and just be with oneself.

Sleep is one process where this takes place, where the mind is stilled from our earthly or worldly actions and activities.

In this context, I am very purposely ignoring the dream state which is not for discussion here.

Some of us have learnt and are able, using forms of meditation, or going into a meditative state, to remain alert to things around us, but also to otherwise take ourselves away from what is going on around us.

Do not ignore this type of thinking or meditative state.

To be with just oneself is an excellent way (either asleep or awake) of overcoming the intensity of daily activities and confrontations.

There is reference to meditative practices later in this book.

With very little practice, regardless of how you do it, you can take yourself into a realm of relative (to you) stillness.

The rewards of stillness or silent contemplation, reflection or meditation, whichever word you wish to use, have been written about by others more knowledgeable than I.

You will, as a result of undertaking some sort of silence activity, (I am avoiding the use of the word meditation) appear to those friends, partners and others who know and respect you, as someone, who has something different (not better) to offer.

Someone who has the ability to "switch off" as occasion demands and thus gain mind sustenance and energy for the ensuing, subsequent daily, mental activities.

As an aside, I doubt that the cup of tea or coffee ritual, on your own, or with a friend, neighbor, worker or family member has ever occurred to most of us as being a concept of that period in the day where we really do not have to think. Where there is very little necessary thought function.

We are just "being" with the other person or persons. We are relaxed, we are rejuvenated, we are able to move on to the next task of the day with renewed energy.

Our ongoing continual thought patterns are an important aspect of who we all are.
You might then question as to how this makes us seem to others.

At the risk of repeating myself:

It is important to know and realise that as an individual, you are a one off. In this world of billions of people, there is no other person with your potential, abilities, knowledge, will to succeed, fear of failure, that who is the same as you.
You can consider, if you wish, that you are respected for your contribution to this world, of yours and ours. You are contributing to the success of humanity, no matter that you think otherwise.

It is appropriate and necessary to say at this point, that there is not much that you do not already know about what I have just said.
You know or realise these things, maybe on a conscious level and/or, also maybe on a level of subconscious realization.

There are lessons to learn, experiences to anticipate, the love of living, the enjoyment of loving and giving to others, being with acquaintances, friends, partners, Mother Earth, and humanity from time to time.

These mentioned and other unmentioned things, are what makes up just who You and I are in this world of ours.

There is so much more to you and me.

And, as I type this, I realise that there are some of you who will reread the last paragraph and disagree with it totally.

If this is the case, for you, I now have a very important question:

"Why are you reading this book?"

Would you really like me to be droll, and/or unexciting?
Would it be in order for me to tell you that you really are OKAY, the way you are?

Should I not expect that from time to time, we all, and I mean ALL, need to be prodded into action of some sort.
The fact that we make no change to our lives, is a personal decision, invariably based on our past, life, and living experiences.

I do not want you to change, if that is your desire.
I am only asking, "How do we show up in life". Not as a question but as a statement.

If you made it necessary for me to ask the above question, the next few paragraphs are especially for you.

The rest of you can read on.

I am sure you have met the someone I am about to write about.

You are sick of lessons!

You do not need any more life experiences!

Life is the pits!

Life is not working for you!

The love of your life does not exist!

You hate gardening, and as for other people, which maybe possibly include your partner, "I just wish they would all just go away and leave me alone!"

The person I am talking about, I have known. That someone who appears, for some reason they themselves can't or won't talk about, to be totally switched off from the world around them, the one they securely live in.

There is a saying that usually explains this type of person. It goes something like;

"They are the only one in step as compared to the rest of us, or, the rest of our, or their world".

I believe we might all have tried, in the past, to make a difference to this person's perspectives, by attempting to give them an explanation about how to do things in a different (better) way.

That is, to do something that might improve (in our opinion) their life, or way of being, alive and contributing to humanity, as seen from their own perspective.

And our thoughts and ideas as presented to them make no difference.
That person talks, relates and understands, in some obscure undefinable help fashion way to others.
And they appear to do so on a general and confrontational way.

You and I see, and know, as we hear their communication (or possible tirade) that the other person has small tiny little sparks of something that might be termed "intuitive light".
Yet they do not see this light and are not willing to change their lot in life. Or, as may be said by others, "To let their light shine".

"Why then, if you are one of these persons, are you still reading this book?"
I ask the same question again?

May I suggest you start again at the beginning of this chapter or section, but before you do, REALLY ask yourself; "How do I "really" appear, or, show up to others, in life and living?"

Relate this question to your true inner self where there is no forgiveness, no pretense, just truth, inner peace and knowledge of your true, real self. "Warts and all".

Having got back this far, for you to answer something maybe like, "I don't care," or, "I don't know." Or, "nobody loves me," will be an untruth. You will not have answered your question to yourself, with anything like honesty.

SO, just for YOU an exercise;

The purpose of this exercise is to allow you the privilege of knowing that there is a friend, neighbor or family member who really respects you the way you are.

They see the good things, and the bad things, from their own very personal perspective, and still they communicate to you or allow you to communicate with them.
Know at this point that the use of the word "them" is very specifically made.

I have not ever met anyone who does not have something to give others.

As you talk to other people, see in yourself those goals that have not been attained and personal experiences you might, (were you game enough) point out to the person with whom you are communicating.
I am in no way suggesting, you point out your personal faults and failings to that other person in this, or these conversations. They are purely your personal thoughts, at this point in time.

To openly voice faults and failings is possibly what psychiatrists are for. That is, if you wish to spend money.
As you converse in your mind, as a thought, see what you have really done in your life.

See the personal, even the very personal, living experiences. See yourself as a person who secretly would like to make a difference, even if it's only just to yourself.

Your world is as you have created it.

All I ask is, that you just start.

"Start what?" you ask?
I and others are unable and should not answer that question.
Just start the new game.
"IT IS A GAME" – And, there are no rules to this game.

Were you aware as a child, in your growing up years, that as you started a game with friends, there were no rules? Neither was there an end result objective.
It was a game with no specific rules.

As rules were introduced to the game it started to become a competition.

I am not asking you to compete, as there is no competition in life and living.
Be yourself.
You ultimately will not change who you are, to be someone, something else, but in your own mind you will be different (not better).

NOW, do something outrageous.
It matters not, that others might think this outrageous act or activity isn't much.
Their thoughts and actions are not your thoughts and actions.

You are an individual.

There is only one of YOU, in this world of billions of people.

That is, if you really want to be different (not better).

The rest, whatever it (or you) might look like, will happen naturally.

You will still be you!

SO! How do you privately think now, that you, might or could, appear to others in life?

For all of us, we have those who love us and wish to be part of our life, which is great.

Love these people with all your heart and soul.

You and they are precious, one on one, to each of the others.

We also have those who wish to have nothing to do with us, and that too is OKAY.

It might also be that we do not wish to associate with some, no matter the reason, because we do not relate to them, nor they to us, and that too is OKAY.

Enjoy the gifts you have, and the gifts that life and your way of living, has given you.

Share with others the gifts you have.

Know that you have worked diligently to be the person you are.

Regardless of how you present yourself to the world, there is the payoff.

The most righteous person in the world will be shunned by some.

The person who is considered a thief and or vagabond will be shunned by some.

You will be shunned by some.

Have personal knowing and knowledge, and realise that this too is OKAY.

Enjoy those who wish to be in your company.

In some subtle way, they and you unknowingly and without the need for thought, contribute to each other.

You are OKAY the way you are.

Believe me!

LEARNING TO LISTEN

As you read this, are you able to go back in time to pick up an abstract thought that occurred at some time in the past? A thought, that seemed to be a good idea, but you've never acted on, or about it.

Where I'm coming from in this chapter is:
"That Thought"

I know, I haven't yet told you what that thought of mine is, but other things are, to my mind, more important to present to you at this point in this book.

I am talking about a particular type of thought.
A thought.
Just one.
A thought that has no reason for its existence.

This could be: A thought that may be something like: "I really like this person."
Or maybe: "What am I doing here." Or maybe also: "He/She seems friendly."

In these instances, it might have occurred at a time you first met someone, and they were introducing themselves.
Or, you find yourself in an unexpected place, maybe, with someone you don't know.

Or, you were learning or being instructed and a stray or abstract thought came into your mind.
Or whatever, or whenever, it doesn't matter!

Are you able to remember that "the thought" came and went in almost a fraction of a second?

You knew at the time that thought was correct, you had no doubt as to its truth and reality, and you most likely ignored it, by being polite.

BUT! Most times, we treat the thought with "ignore" and get on with what we are doing.

This is the type of thought that can create in its very brief existence a subtle change in our lives or our way of being. Where it, as a singular thought, impacts on how we perceive ourselves, and/or relate to others.

The reason I ask the question is, that all of us continue to allow our own thoughts to intrude when someone is talking, speaking, or relating something to us.

It might be a personal conversation with someone you know, or someone you have just met, a speaker from a rostrum, or an overheard conversation.

We are all guilty of this! Not like guilty as something bad, but guilty as something we maybe shouldn't do. But we do anyway.

As we listen, the thought(s) drop in, and well before the other person has finished what they were saying - we might, or want, to interrupt.

Our personal thought is (to ourselves) more important than what the other person is saying, or the discourse we are listening to.

Specifically, in relation to a personal or group conversation, the speaker is interrupted by you, or someone who wants to get their "Two Bobs", worth in."
(the term, "Two Bobs Worth" is an Old English term, meaning the interrupting of a lecture or conversation, to have your say – (which most times is irrelevant)

Is this because our personal knowledge or observation on the particular conversational subject has not been covered?
Is this because we are impatient and have to have our say?
Is this because, in our opinion the thought we have, is more important than that which is being presented?
Is this because we don't want to hear any more of that which was being presented?
Is this because we have heard it all before and can't be bothered hearing it again?
Is it because we will not wait our turn to speak, because the point of view we have at that moment will be irrelevant later on in the conversation?

Or is it just because we just can't be bothered listening to someone else talking, when we personally know we already have the answers, and our way is going to be the best. (Not better nor different). This is regardless, of anyone else's opinion or way of doing things.

Possibly it might be all of these things, none of these things, or something else.

Of all of you reading this, there will be very few, who have not been on some sort of committee, board, or part of a discussion group.

You will know exactly what I am saying with regard to interrupting a speaker in the middle of their conversation or presentation of thoughts and ideas.

Even worse, how many times has that interruption resulted in many conversations going on at the same time, where it is impossible to hear and know what is being discussed, and where there is definitely no possible consensus.

Personally, I have over the years, learnt to sit and be quiet, and be patient.

I know there will be no point in joining in. It won't make any difference.

Fortunately, there comes a point in all discussions, where and when all things are more or less covered, and consensus does takes place.

We will, as a group of individuals, compromise on our personal thought patterns and create personal consensus, so we can move on.

There will come a time in every conversation, when the subject has been "talked to death".

There is nothing more that can be added, and the only way to move on to something else is to compromise.

Do we "really listen", to those who communicate to us?
Most times I think not! At least not always.
Do those to whom we communicate really listen to us?
Again, I think not. They certainly won't tell you so.

Therein is a conundrum with regard to the previous chapter. If I am right, in that we as individuals do not listen, - we hear, but that is not listening. Thus, how can it be that verbal communication between individuals really does exist, and has very traceable and positive end results.

For you the reader, and I as the author a couple of questions:
"My thought pattern must exist so that I can absorb that which is being related to me?"
"I have questions, because a particular item was presented that was beyond my understanding."

To interrupt what I am saying or alluding to at this point, in the narration.

I am not here referring to gossip.
Gossip is always about negative things. It is never about the positive side of people or activities.
Gossip is talking about someone else, or other people, or activities, where that or those being discussed are not privy to the conversation.
They have no right of communication to validate the accuracy of what is being stated, or that which is invariably an untruth, or at the very least, not accurate.

Know that: people that gossip, also usually embellish that which was passed on to them.

I personally do not tolerate and will walk away from gossip.
I also achieve this by interrupting as soon as I can, and sooner if possible, and terminate that person's speaking.
When I am told that what is being given me is important information, I request the speaker go back to whomsoever they are talking about and have them communicate to me the particular subject matter.
Needless to say, this never happens.

Additionally, there is the circumstance when one will be asked what to do when someone you know, tells you they have/has heard gossip about themselves.
My advice, when confronted with this, is to advise that friend, acquaintance or family member to completely ignore that which they discovered about themselves.

Some of us find this difficult to do.
This is because our integrity appears to have been compromised.
In this instance, if the person genuinely feels aggrieved, and finds it difficult or impossible to ignore the possible insult, my advice is to go back to the person, who related what is really gossip, and have them go back to their informer with a request to confront the person. That is, the person who they were talking about.
This also never happens.
Not another word is said or repeated.

An aspect of communication amongst the younger generation is the art of whispering supposed secrets.

Girls tend to do this more than boys, who tend to speak out, regardless of who is present.

As we grow older, there is more of a tendency to tell secrets one on one, privately.

This occurs when we meet with friends and family and do not have to whisper.

When we see people whispering to each other there is always a tendency by those present to want to know what is being whispered.

And whispering is always gossip.

The best way to handle gossip is to ignore it!

Especially if you really know your integrity and honesty are intact.

Let us move on!!

I am reminded of a game we used to play as children, say at a party where there may be something like ten people present. The object is to whisper in the ear of the person next to you a four-word statement, and ask that person to pass on the four words, also by whispering.

The four words can be repeated if the listener doesn't hear them properly the first time. Some people just don't whisper clearly, which sometimes creates a problem in communication. The last person states that which was whispered into their ear.

Never, have those been the same,

And, invariably there are more or less words at the end.

In this example there could be a number of aspects present:

The way we listen - hearing what is said - so it can be remembered;

Hearing what is said, and thinking about remembering it;

Remembering to speak those exact words;

The thought of the ability to whisper properly, that is, loudly enough for the person to hear but softly enough so nobody else hears;

PLUS, lots of other personal thoughts which come into play at the same time as you are whispering the four (maybe more or less) words.

Overriding all things, which does not help, are our thoughts of "getting it right", not only be the communicator, but also by the listener.

Something that becomes more important is "will we remember."

The fact that we don't remember the exact words appears to be a normal human ability.

On a slightly different subject, I personally have a high regard for those people who can remember and repeat a joke.

Apart from the fact that I have no ability to present jokes in a suitable manner, I have the ability to stuff up by having my own conversation on remembering. The salient points of the joke go missing, and presentation is truly, impossibly lost.

Maybe one day I might have a conversation with one of these joke tellers to see how they firstly remember, then-------. Forget it. It's never going to happen.

To get back to where I was before:

We think we are hearing that which is being presented to us. Our hearing however is invariably mixed up and interspersed with our own thoughts, and thinking.

If we are in some sort of altered or meditative state, we will not be hearing, or maybe hearing but not perceiving that which is being said.

As was said before, this is a way to still thought patterns.

All of us know it is useless to say something to someone who is asleep.

Our continual, personal, thought process, interrupts invariably, and all the time.

Recently I was required to present a difficult matter to a prominent government departmental employee. I took the time to carefully present, lay out, and explain the problem.

To then be asked by the person who answered the phone, a question that clearly informed me they had not heard my first words, let alone the rest of the statement.

My only option at that point was to request the listener to have my conversation. "Listen to what I am saying. Do not have your own conversation at the same time as I am talking."

Believe me! I didn't have to repeat myself or any part of the presentation a third time.

I am sure I am not alone on this one, as it has happened many, many times over many years of necessary communication to government authorities.

Thankfully most of you are more tolerant than I, and you are prepared to repeat your statement.

And I am as guilty as that government employee, in doing the same thing!

In my professional career I have been privy to many conversations. These range around technical business observations, decisions and questions.

It often occurs that statements of a very personal nature are made in the middle of a technical or business discussion.

It is obvious that that speaker has not been concentrating on the points of the discussion, but who is going to do the job being discussed.

Here we possibly or probably have to be a little more careful. Are we going to hear gossip, or is the communicator specifically in awe of what needs to be said and/or done, and wishes to communicate something about themselves, or another member present?

You might say here, that I have digressed somewhat from my topic of "Learning to listen"

But, listening takes many forms.

Listening to, listening about, listening by subterfuge, spying, and so on.

They are all important aspects of how we live our everyday lives.

Even a deaf person, who cannot hear the spoken word, but understands what is being said or presented, by signing or lip reading, will have the same aspects of the thought process when communication takes place.

We learn by listening. Only by the simple aspect of concentrating wholly on what is being said.

When someone speaks in our presence – are we able to listen and learn without our own thoughts intruding?.

I really do mean, that you concentrate, ONLY on what is being said.

Sure, your own thoughts continue to occur, but you become duty bound, in your own mind, not to mentally interrupt and listen.

At committee meetings, you will find that when this takes place in your personal world of communication, things start to open up.

This is because the person communicating has the chance to really cover all aspects of that which is being said, and communicated.

Give yourself the opportunity to listen to a question/answer session in parliament, as presented on television!

It takes a very good chairperson at a meeting to only have one person speak at any time. Those meetings are enjoyable.

With the ongoing technological changes continually taking place in our lives, it is becoming more and more important that we all hear the communications taking place.

This, in my opinion, is vitally important with regard to our learning more about things electronic.

There is no reason to feel inadequate because you are not up to date.

There is also no reason to feel inadequate because you have no wish to learn the new electronic means of communication, or for that matter, anything new.

But – what is your safeguard, in any conversation, words are secretly being recorded.
Beware of this at meetings!

At the same time, "seek and you will receive".
Ask questions, and you will be rewarded with answers.
If you do not understand the answers, communicate your inability to understand.

Most people love to help other people.
If there is someone who can't be bothered with you, thank them anyway, and move on.

Maybe it was not your time to learn something new!

That "thought" where I started at the beginning of this book.

It is still there. It is complete. It remains in the memory banks complete.

You can recall it at will.
It will not desert you.

AND
No – you haven't yet been informed.
This chapter was about "Learning to Listen" not "That Thought"

Interlude and Philosophy

Learning to listen, was only intended to be somewhat akin to "that thought".
I mentioned it in passing and didn't get any further.

I had intended a discussion on thoughts that occur in our lives, such as "That Thought", and the actions and activities that might, or could most possibly, probably, result from putting "that thought", to good (hopeful)use.
And now, in my personal living situation, it's sort of, ended up om a "back burner", to quote a saying used in Australia, where something is intended to be complete, but, just doesn't seem to get to completion.

The previous chapters, and maybe, possibly yours too, are about my personal journey through life.

Where we are, in the personal perspective, of life, and living!

We are all in this big wide wonderful world of ours "LIVING AND LEARNING".

What I have not said is, "To learn things, one has just to listen."

I am not talking here, with the learning requirement, and need, to manipulate tools, materials, electronics, machines, computers, and yes, that new mobile phone.

And, I would also add, reading this whole "The Way We Are".

Just as importantly, these chapters, and my writings, are **only**, a lead in, to a different learning process.

The "ART" of sharing, somewhat akin to discussion, but by hearing the spoken word as part of listening to what is said, discussed, thought about, and listening.

To my mind, his is becoming a somewhat lost human, shall we say. ART.
With the advent of computer driven technology.
I say this, because of the introduction of electronics as applied to technology.
Mainly, that development of the telephone, that no longer sits on a shelf or bench, as it did so for many, many years – most times ignored till it rang.

"The Computer commenced a different aspect of communication – then Emails appearing at about the same time – and the mobile telephone, rapidly moving from "The Brick" to what it is today, and who knows what, into the immediate future.
Apps, and other technologies, becoming an integral part of what is now deemed appropriate and totally necessary and present, no matter where you may be.
Then as texting, almost demanding immediate attention, and response, for those of us who are older, the "Dick Tracey", of the comic books, and his wrist watch, which gave him the ability to communicate by voice, wherever & whenever!

One can, in this day and age, only wonder as what might or may be next.

Perhaps eliminate paper, and create a situation where this document, in electronic form, will be present with you all the time – to refer to "ad lib".
Let us also at the same time, also eliminate the "Contents" listing as redundant too.

As an older member of our civilization, I am at a loss, to anticipate, in any way or form, the future of past well known applications, as to what was then, and at this time, effective verbal communication.
This also will, to my way of thinking, have many applications to life, living, communication, relationships, education and learning, and, who could know what else at the time of composing this missive.

I have somewhat digressed – so be it.

In using the word "listening", I am inferring, that each and every one of us, listens, but, at the same time, creates a mental response to what is being said, or related.

Thus, each and every on of us, may be deemed "a listener", and, "a creator", all the time.

And know, that discussion which is purely aimed at personal concepts, personal ideas, the sharing of thoughts and concepts, can and also is, the way to real learning.
Why else, do we have schools and universities?

As you and I go through life, we continue to learn.
Not necessarily big things, or important things, but maybe little snippets from here and there.

That I get to be diverted on a continual basis from my perceived – (I know but really don't know where I am, which equals unknown) purpose in life, is about living the opportunities that present themselves hour by hour, or more than likely – day, week, month, year.

What a great world we live in!
The opportunity to present one's concepts and ideas!

That "thought" is still important in the scheme of things, and the telling.
I will get to it eventually.

In the meantime, before I continue the journey, which I trust you too will continue with me, there is something I wish to introduce!

―――――――――――――

There is an ancient Philosophy, which I believe to be Chinese. In my reading and studies over the years, I have found some references and similar evidence in various other religious practices.

This philosophy divides life experiences into periods of threes and sevens.

The first period of the three, is LEARNING!

The second period of the three, is putting into PRACTICE, the LEARNING!

The third period of the three, is relationships!

The three periods are divided into periods of SEVEN years each.

The THREE is mandatory!

BUT, the SEVEN YEAR PERIOD, can vary from say SIX to EIGHT years.

This twenty-one-year cycle, of the three times seven, can also vary, very slightly.

And will, regardless of any other set of circumstances, realign itself, at a future time, well before death.

A child, up to the age of seven, is learning.

Learning to walk, talk, relate, be independent.

BUT: ignore in the context of this writing; the current trend of child-care and its social and learning ramifications, and maybe, to a lesser extent, pre-school learning.

Whilst, in this day and age, they are a fact of life, I am sure there are other writings about this current trend of the human race, to create knowledge and acceptability.

Many discussions with others, have also indicated there is little, if any, impact on this original age-old concept

Learning takes many forms, in many varying different ways and because we are ALL totally individual, we all learn in different mental ways.

The variation in the seven years, to maybe six, or eight years, can be used as an example, by many people.

As an example, it is well known that girls learn faster than boys in certain areas, and at certain ages.

The second seven years, is putting the previously learnt principles into action. This is where children are taught the art and ramifications of listening and paying attention.

The initial learning phase of the first seven years is put to use. For some, this is used effectively, and for some, the time is more or less wasted.

I am here, not only referring to school work.

Relationships, well and truly come into play between the ages of eight and fourteen.

However, as we recall our growing up years to some extent, we remember we are different. Thus, different lessons are learnt and remembered.

As adults, the concept of learning at school is deemed very important.

But, we all know of children, who don't or refuse to learn at school.

And, we also know of those who are successful in later life, even though they didn't finish formal schooling.

As for myself, you may ask, but I believe, at this time in my life, the answer, either way, is totally irrelevant.

A question. Are older children actually, on a conscious level, putting into practice, the learning of the first seven years of life?

Therein, for some of us, there is now possibly another subject to explore.

At this time, as technology is coming to the fore, is the time for discussion somewhere else, by people more expert than me.

The third set of seven years, occurs at around the age of fourteen, as children reach puberty. There is an evident change, in the way life experiences eventuate.

These are the relationship years.

Where, real first-time love appears, when young adults really start to explore their sexuality, when youth really learns the application of their true identity, and the value of friendships. When, the true friendships are created. Some of these friendships lasting a lifetime.

And then – The three by seven-year cycle starts again.

As an aside, have a quick think about the well-known: "Seven Year Itch"

Modern living, appears to have changed this twenty-one-year cycle somewhat.

But it is ironical that university study usually finishes at the age of twenty-eight.

And advertisements for senior staff, indicate an age of less than thirty-five.

Marriage and those relationships, appear to have a slightly different perspective.

I mention the Seven Year Itch above, but also appear to fail during the fourteen to twenty-one-year period, or when partner is in the thirty-five to forty-two-year age group

And, because forty, is so close to forty-two, who wants to get past forty and have to start learning again?

That, dear reader, is the way it is!

For myself, I am in a relationship cycle, (some 33 plus years), and in just over a year ahead I return to the learning cycle once again!

One can only wonder, what the future may bring to account. As stated somewhere else: "On With the Motley"

Each and every one of us is aware that there are many ways of looking at life, many philosophies for us to study, if we desire, many paths to follow, in our living and learning.

Regardless of which study for truth and understanding is undertaken, the principles continue to apply.

I mention this particular philosophy because it is so easy to remember.

It is also an interesting, unobtrusive trail to follow, both with friends, family members and acquaintances.

Give it a try, and see how accurate it can be, in its own simple way.

The Impetuosity of Youth

We were all young once.
Do you remember?
Do you choose not to remember?

.

Personally, I prefer to remember.
Playing with my brother under the lemon tree, in the dirt, in
our back yard, losing upper front teeth by tripping over my
bike. making Bows and Arrows to play with, playing Goodies
and Baddies, my personal shanghai, playing down the park,
checking out the interior of the old sewerage works chambers;
and a lot more stuff that probably should never be mentioned
or remembered.
There are many reasons why, either or in some instances,
both answers are appropriate.
You might now ask; "But how is it that both answers can be
appropriate."

Think back, to some event that took place, say in your teen
years, or maybe sooner if you desire.
If you are still a teenager reading this, think back to a time
before you entered those teen years.

Keep in mind, at all times, that we are all individuals.
And know that, no two people in the world, will remember
events in exactly the same way.

Those "angels" among us ordinary people will immediately think of the good things they did as teenagers and/or younger members of our world.

The rest of us! "WELL?"

I don't believe I was an "angel", BUT THEN:
There are those of us, who at times, or at that time knew they were on an adventure. Sometimes, it was the intention, by demonstration and noise, to wake up ordinary people to do something that needed changing.

At the same time, the rest of us will hone in on the irrational or stupid activities we managed to achieve with some form of success, and possible angst to others.

Or, maybe you immediately brought to mind all, or some, or one of these events, things in your youth, that you have possibly never shared with anybody else.

Take a few moments to recall and look back, from your life as you see it now, to the years of that time, in your youth.

For younger readers, perhaps those under 18 years of age or whatever, your memories of recent events should/will immediately come to mind.

As you think back, and recall, attempt to see, or experience, the emotional thought(s) that stirred your inner being, at the time you were doing, or thinking, those things.

Your memories should and/or can immediately hone in, on the reasoning you had in your mind, as to why those thoughts/activities were undertaken.

Immediately tune into that "personal inner sense" of maybe doing and achieving something different.

At the same time, doing what might be called senseless activities; and, did you engage in sense of being different, and showing the world that it was going to be so.

Tune in mentally, to the memories, of the energy you had, the energy you were prepared to demonstrate, to all and sundry. Did you have, your own personal intention of communicating to every person who came into contact with you, your activities?

If you did, or didn't, at his time, is immaterial.

Your parents, logically would come first.

But then, that might mean some form of being chastised.

The fact that you did or didn't is of importance or otherwise as you recall or remember the emotion of the activity.

I don't want to know what or whatever. "Just asking".

AND:

There are those of you reading this, who will have no desire whatsoever, to go back into that period in their life, that period to which I have just made reference – being your youth, teenage years or younger.

The events and things that took place then, for you, "ARE A NO GO AREA".

At the time, or later in life, you made the decision that those events be forgotten.

They have ALWAYS been this way, and will remain so, for as long as you live.

I accept this attitude without question, as I have friends and acquaintances, with the same view of their past.

At the same time, my request is to be patient with this written word.

Fortunately, in this earthy world in which we reside, there is always the opportunity to be different.
Thank goodness!

Please, be patient with me and my written word.

I ask this, as I Believe and know that your past is part of who you are, and to ignore your past is an act of attempting to ignore yourself.

You, I, and the rest of humanity, are who you are.
It is not possible to ignore yourself, and I am sure you realise this instinctively.

There is one human nature type, that occurs for lots of personal reasons. The quiet type.
This is in the main, the person who would have liked to change things from the way they were, to something else.
For lots of reasons, this didn't eventuate or happen.
Those "lots of reasons" might cover things like domination, abuse, intolerance, neglect, ignorance, prejudice; just to name a few.

You, possibly or maybe, being one of these people, went along with the "status quo", didn't upset people.

You just got on with what had to be done, did what ever had to be done quietly, without fuss.

Sometimes, you might have decided you would like to be prompted, maybe to just to let people know you existed.

Keep the peace! Your peace! It was/is simpler that way!

And in reading that statement, you could ask; "What else could you be but be human".

I leave you, the reader, to decide in your own mind, which trait you believe yourself to be.

Whilst at the same time, you would be entitled to dismiss the word "trait".

On my own personal level, as I write these words, I regard my own life as being one of living and learning, with the ups and downs of life such as they are.

I leave you, the reader, to decide in your own mind which one you believed, or at this current time, believe and/or know, yourself to be.

And, it most likely is one of those I have just mentioned. And that too is OK.

If you allow, you may now get a quiet realization why your youth was an important aspect of who you were at the time, and its relative value to your present personality.

I totally assure you all again, that your youth, (the term I will use from now on to cover all those other words), and the way you lived, was, and is, part of the many determining factors which make up the person you are, "NOW".

Our living past is one of the bases on which we have ALL, without exception, built our present lives, and way of "being", which is another word for "living".

"Being", is a word I prefer to use, as we acknowledge ourselves as human beings.

In a subtle way, I have referred to this aspect of our living experiences in previous pages, and it will come up again as we progress, through this publication.

Generally, the youth of this world always seem to love experimenting.
They appeal to the love and the concept of changing things, are seemingly impatient with things the way they are, want to make changes, only for the sake of change, with end results, that appear to have no purpose. That is, no purpose when viewed by members of the older generation.
Many times, it seems, that the younger generation want change only for change's sake.

Previously, I mentioned the fourteen to twenty-one-year age group, the youth of this, our world, who are in the relationship cycle.
In this activity, as part of that relationship cycle, is also the subtle desire, to create.

To create a relationship with their "living" world, the world that they perceive they don't want to be part of, or want to change, as it exists around them.

Generally, the personal investigation of our world around us, our relationship with it, our specific relationship with nature and natural things, seems to come into being, sometime after puberty starts.
That is – after the learning cycle;
And, the putting into practice, those learnings.

What takes place in the minds of youth?
What is it that determines, for many of our youth, our younger generation,
That the way things are, ARE NOT OK?
What is it that those youthful youth energies seek change?
Regardless, of how stable the world appears to us, the older generation?
Were you, in your younger days, one of those people who demanded change, change for change's sake?
But, did not believe this possible to you, in the eyes of the older generation.

As a male, being much older now, than the current youth generation, which I live and associate with, and the many various technical, electronic, opportunities, learning, ability implications, readily available, receiving and passing on of information, etc., which were not there as I grew up, could if I chose, make me feel somewhat isolated.
In fact, I do not wish to be isolated, as a member of the older generation.

To be able to communicate, and have that younger life attitude and knowledge, passed on to me, I consider a privilege.
This works for me and that person, because it is and remains a discussion.
There is no right, there is no wrong, just conversation.

My current living world, is so very different, to that which it was in my youth, and the times I am referring to previously.

Change, I am not totally familiar with, has eventuated.
And, it is nothing like that, which I may have thought logical those many, many years ago.

I have no intention of identifying the many and various generational activity changes that have appeared, then disappeared again.
Names given to whatever have come into being as part of our daily lives, and, now no longer exist.

Am I referring to the fact that rapid change is now a state of being, created by the impetuosity of youth, the vibrational effects, now showing up in our world?

Am I now alluding to the fact that there has been some kind of generational change, which quite possibly make previous earthly living concepts outdated, as Mother Earth moves out of, to some new generational, world learning period?
And, should I make these questions into statements?

I have mentioned before, that a created game remains a game, if there are no rules.

Is this the youthful enthusiasm, vibrational thought activity, that is creating that game change, in our current lifetime?

Yes, it is a question, to which I do not believe I could choose an answer.
And, I ask at the same time;
"Are there amongst us, those in the youth arena who do have that impetuosity".

On a very personal basis, much as I find current technology difficult to apply and contend with;
"SO BE IT"

INTERLUDE

As I was concluding the previous chapter on youth, it occurred to me to specifically include something, for the younger members of our world community, say, the time before becoming a teenager.

To explain;
The chapters making up this whole missive of so many possible and/or probable life sequences, or, parts of those life sequences, to some extent, and from my very personal thinking, appear or tend to possibly be, somewhat biased.
That is, biased towards the older generations, in this world in which we live.

As I was concluding the previous chapter on youth, it occurred to me to specifically include something, for the younger members of our world community, say, the time before becoming a teenager.

And, at the same time, as I was reviewing, this previous chapter based on youth, I sensed a bias, that was never intended.
To the point that, the chapter following this interlude, has been totally segregated from the initial draft of the whole document.
It was a subconscious thought that was definitely not intended.

This thought was about the world's rapid uptake of new technology and its ever-ongoing manifestations, mainly based, but not exclusively, on electronics and communication technology.

More or less at the same time, I became mentally aware that whilst my whole life and living experiences, have been based on a very subtle and personal what's next, how can humanity, really improve its way of being human, throughout the whole world.

What could be done to create a wholeness of life to each and every living thing on this planet?
Not as a question that was going to get an immediate answer or resolution.
But something like, will all this new and ongoing new technology, the like of which has never been experienced before on Mother Earth:
Give humanity, the opportunity to be at one with itself, the whole world over?

Our Younger Generation

In alluding to the words "younger generation", it is intended as being basically, from birth to teenage years, that is, to about when the word teenager, comes into use.

Keep in mind, that there is no specific date, or published specific data, that applies to the naming and using such words, as might apply to the word "youth".

As our children grow up, in their own individual and particular way, they create for themselves, a glimpse, of what may be their future life experiences.

Of importance to notice, how actions, thinking, and being older matures, probably best done by most of us, in bringing back personal memories, from those same years.

"BUT"; how times have changed.

Information and its availability to the very young, and the younger children, in this day and age, is so different in this present time, almost to the point of, there is no specific data to create a comparison.

Or, to compare information and data available today, to each one of us, as was available, say some 10 or so years ago, would be like comparing chalk and cheese.

There is no it. Whatever the "it was or is" becomes an irrelevant point of view, like, "It was what I did", (or didn't) do, from an adult.

All the growing up child will hear is, something, you did, some time ago.

Your memories are just that.

Set their young world, by whom you are, and your personal actions, on a day to day way of living, and discreet activities.

As adults, we have learnt and know, that human life and events have occurred in some obscure, totally indefinable way.

Sure, you could go back and recall small things changing, that is, as you remember them, but what is the point, the young mind is not party to your memories.

Some of us applaud the activities of these new and recent member(s) of our family.

At the same time, it is more than quite possible, things are viewed with anything between amusement, dismay, disgust, couldn't care less, denial, or whatever, by the younger generation.

At this point I am only going to refer to my mother, bringing myself and my brother up, in my childhood. Dad, as a result of 1st war injuries, was not able to cope with or children's perceived misbehavior

I know, rather than presume, coming from my own and my brother's very clear childhood memories, of mother's nonchangeable instructions and attitude, but, not including children should be seen and not heard; to behave and learn, understand and realise, gain knowledge by listening, and behave; that the gems of wisdom, coming from adult conversations, we were sometimes allowed to hear, have remained with us for the whole of our lives.

Absolute integrity and honesty, all the time, is an absolute must.

Another must, is to be truthful and honest, with integrity, all the time.

I can still remember times, when mother was caught out doing something I or my brother considered naughty.

An explanation was always forthcoming without denial.

But, most importantly for us, was an explanation of adult reasoning, and explanations.

I am certain, and my brother is in total agreement, that mum's total honesty with us at all times, flowed into our own lives, as having the base, for our own desire to have that same high level of integrity and honesty.

I am, in presenting this tid-bit of my family way of life, trusting it will assist you, the reader.

No, in many ways, I have no desire to be called a saint.

Life is for living, making mistakes, sometimes being devious, hiding things in the back yard so mum wouldn't find out, (and if she did, never told us.)

(I wonder if they are still there to-day, where we grew up, some 1,000Km away.

In my previous chapter, the "Impetuosity of Youth", I was alluding more to the age group, more possibly starting somewhere round 12 plus years of age.

Yes, I know, that maybe some people never, or take a long time to "grow up".

And, I could have been one of those people, except that financial problems reared their ugly head when I was fifteen. Mum got some information, that the Australian Navy were looking for youngsters, my age, to become instrumentalists, and more or less enrolled me for some seven and a half years. As it happens, it was the best thing. All of a sudden, I had to grow up quickly.
And, that was the start of the best years of my life for the next twelve years, of which seven years were spent at sea, as part of the Admiral's Band.

Enough of me!
But, it is of some importance to know and realise, that as parents, and/or adults, friend or acquaintance, grand parent, uncle or aunt, whomsoever; by example, the young and very young can know and understand, in their own time, integrity, whatever that word implies to yourself, the reader.

It is interesting to realise that, there are members of the older generation, who are very capable of enlisting our younger generation, our youth, in some way or fashion.
I do totally respect, the person who is able to make their very particular passion or individual thought, come into realization.

Somewhere before this, I think I mentioned somewhere, the term "business as usual".
I am this time, referring to the fact that learning, is something that takes place, either naturally or by requirement.

If it is by requirement, say for a school exam, many times it is something, later on totally discarded as useless knowledge. It gave me no lasting advantage.

As I write this, I automatically sift my mind into our current life and learning arena; yes! "Technology has made that one totally obsolete".

Youth, can seemingly see, at times, into the thinking of us, their older generation.

Listen in a polite manner and do nothing.

At this point, I maybe repeating something I said in either of, "The imperiousity of youth", and or, this chapter, "Our younger generation"

Maybe, each and every one of us, from the youngest to the oldest reader of this document, should look back on the past, and view as a distant memory, the then existing, "Winds of Change."

Something like?

The power the youth of this, "our world", has in its hands.

Youth, acting on its own, and possibly in a separate, particular way.

Youth, continuing to achieve, whatever that may look like.

What would it look like, if we were all, as humanity, able to be younger again, or have younger memory abilities, to do the things we did, as that "younger generation"?

Would we still be able, (as the older members of society), to make a difference?

Or, is it easier to conform, follow the rules of society, such as they are. Rules we know work, work without effort or thought, which makes life relatively, pleasant and enjoyable.

Is it right that we become complacent?
As we grow older, because it is easier to conform to established laws and/or procedures, the rules of the community, in which we live, or, some other rules?

I WONDER!

Relationships

Almost invariably, when one comes into a discussion with someone else on relationships, the personal thought of those partaking in that discussion turn to their own, very current situation.

On a personal level, I truly believe I am the luckiest person in the world to have my wife, as my companion in my present living experience.
A person I trust without question, my current partner in my life experiences.

Incidentally, my wife trusts me just as totally.

On a wider level, I have friends and clients who respect and trust me – regardless of my personality traits.
For this I am grateful.

Internationally, I would wish I were more tolerant of certain countries and their ways of living.
Specifically, as regards differences, the variations of the ways, of how things are done and completed in the country in which I live, as compared to those countries, whoever they may be.

Do I, or should we, assume, that our relationship, or relationships, with those close to us, and those we have never met, be, more or less, one and the same.

If, and when viewed, from a personal perspective on how we are, as members of the human race?

I personally do not think this is the case.

Just something to think about!

Regarding our own county, city, community, neighbors, family, friends and so on to community casual, occasional, in passing, and, ---- etc. etc.

Each individual, as part of this discussion, may or could be, married, have a partner, be engaged, be in a casual relationship, be divorced, looking for a partner, or decidedly single, or friendly, casual, whatever.
I trust I have covered you all, relationship wise.

Another member of this discussion might be a younger person, someone who has not at this time in their life, considered themselves a member of a family, as being in some form of relationship via a family unit, such as it may be.

Notwithstanding, what I am about to say might be appropriate in many family situations.

Where I am coming from at this point in time, is the apparent disintegration of the family unit, as an underlying past concept, of the total welfare family unit, or unit of earlier communities.

There is, to my mind, a conundrum here with regard to modern family living.

Please be patient with me on this point, as I am not implying that the world's families are going in this or any other direction.

But, there is a conundrum here with regard to what is considered, modern day living.

I am here, referring to the ever-current increase in technology, which at this time is having the effect of diversifying family members, into separate identities.

Technology appears to be diminishing the "old fashioned" way of the creation family bonding.

Does this also apply to other non-family type relationship?

Or, put another way, computers and mobile phones, with the social applications for the passing on of information, and its deemed necessity to immediately reply or respond, appears to be overtaking the desire to communicate effectively in some instances, on a face to face level.

Not so long ago, TV was being blamed in much the same fashion.

One might then ask, "Is this the way of the future?

The, what might be termed, old-fashioned family unit, was there for its family members, regardless of the events in the community, or the world.

But, as I ask this question, I do appreciate that there have always been very cohesive families, what might in the past and maybe the present, been called ordinary families and also broken or maybe dysfunctional families.

In all instances, there is, when one or more members of that family, might do their own thing, quite separately, from the desires of the family unit.

I have devoted the first part of this chapter to some aspects of family relationships, as I believe this is the arena whereby the individual, as they grow older, learns by example, from the older generation, the value of a relationship.

Is the growing up of each of us, within the family unit, the means whereby we as individuals, learn in some way how to create, foster and continue, any one, or many particular or passing relationships?

Know, that in reality relationships, take many different forms for each and every individual in this world of ours.

As an example, consider the relationship the country in which you live, may have, with any one of the numerous other countries in this world.

Or, following on that line of thought.
While we are considering our country to other countries in the world; is there any correlation with regard to family relationships and world relationships?

Presuming you consider yourself a permanent resident, or native of your country, you will have specific loyalties about the place where you live.

This, could be from your own personal perspective, the town, the state or county, the country, and also maybe, the rest of the world.

Your sense of relationship will differ as you view or consider other environments or countries in the world.
But just as important, is the view you have of those making up the population of your own country.

Because we are many individuals, we have our governments, parliaments, presidents, and others who act on our behalf in relation to all the other countries in the world.

Thus, to some extent, the relationship you personally have in your mind, may possibly exist by virtue of your opinions about how your country relates to other countries, as well as, your upbringing in your family unit.

I suppose, from my own thinking at this point in time, I might now have an opinion or perspective that will pertain to the next chapter, tolerance.

To continue on:
We all have relationships that continue, start and finish on a continuing and everlasting part of our life's' experiences.

Where and how do our relationships come into existence?
Why do they continue – sometimes for a lifetime?
Why do we vow, on having a good time with someone else over a short period, to be their friend and then have nothing come of that vow?

Why do relationships end, and what makes the conclusion occur?

You the reader, may have valid personal answers to these questions, and probably some questions I did not ask.

You may have answered these and other questions with a personal "so be it".

You may have decided, in some fashion that you made an incorrect assumption on a possible future friendship, and it did not come about.

You may still be pondering the why, of your not continuing the relationship or friendship.

At the same time, for our own very personal reasons, we decide to end the relationship without any communication to the other person or persons.

May we pursue some possible answers together.
I personally believe, that as we look back on these questions, and possibly those, or some other questions, we automatically know the answer.

This might, or may be, because we have moved on in some way wherein our lives, loves, manners and possibly circumstances somehow changed.

I leave it to you to have and trust your personal opinion and reasoning.

Circumstances, of an as yet unknown quality or quantity, may or could, possibly in time, create a rethink on a previous decision.

The freedom of choice, is for each and every one of us a treasure, to adhere to.

Yet, at the same time, not totally or specifically with regard to this topic:
Request a friend, family member, family, stranger, whomsoever, for help, in the decision-making process.

There could, would, maybe, be the eventual decision, lots of us have never looked into, at to determine where we would, or maybe where we would stand, with regard to declaring a long-lasting friendship or relationship, no longer exists.

And on reading the previous paragraphs you might realize I have dropped in the word friendship.

This then poses the question of determining the degree of separation on the difference between those two words:
Relationship and Friendship

Which then poses the question:
Can you have a friendship with a relation?
Can you have a relationship with a friend?

May I start with the first question?

I have heard many times over the past few years, that as an adult, it is important for a parent to have their children be their "friends".

As a parent I educated my children in family ways, the best I knew how.

They are now all grown up and have children of their own.

I would be presumptuous in even thinking or remotely considering, I might even think of asking them, "Was I a friend,"

My reasoning at this time in my life, on my own and my children's lives, is that I was their father, no more, no less.

I achieve nothing by asking the question and the answer will be irrelevant.

At the same time, is humanity changing its attitudes in family relationships in this current age, which makes the word "friend" now more appropriate?

I leave you the reader to make a personal determination on that question.

Are friendships and relationships the same thing?

Personally, and thankfully, at this time in my life, I do not even have to consider answering that question.

But, from my scant knowledge of older English Ancestry, it might have been a very legitimate question and answer, to consider.

And the second question:

It goes without saying that very many friendships develop into relationships.

That, some of these relationships do not continue, is not part of this discussion, as mentioned before

I started this chapter with the heading of relationship.
And I have sort of finished on friendship.

It is interesting to my mind, without going to a dictionary to determine their exact meanings, that they are, or almost, exactly the same thing.

The familiarity or love that one human being has for another, be they male or female, who are attracted to each other for some reason or another.
Is it a friendship, that develops into a relationship, that then develops into love?

Is my heading in need of a change in wording?.

Forgive me for not taking this topic further.
It is getting too convoluted.

I leave you, he reader, to follow your own path of research, on this one.

GO WITH LOVE!

HONOUR THAT FRIENDSHIP! – (NOT - HONOUR THE FRIENDSHIP!)

HONOUR THAT RELATIONSHIP

Morals Morality and Integrity

Morals, morality and integrity are ideals that could, or more importantly, should be applied to current very personal society attitudes.

Are they good?
Are they bad?
Are they right?
Are they wrong?

These questions are asked, by all of us, from time to time.

I am referring here, more to an aspect of a conversational topic, rather than a questioning of one's personal attitude to possible life and living actions and activities.

BUT; maybe I'm not!
Because, I personally choose not to venture into, or be part of these conversations.

Some definitions. From my Oxford dictionary – (1934 edition)
MORAL   Power of distinguishing between right and wrong:
MORALITY   Moral principles, Moral conduct:
INTEGRITY   Uprightness, Honesty:

You might question the why, of this topic being part of "The Way We Are"

And, you may absolutely raise this question, as it is very definitely a "lifeblood" in how each and every one of us is seen, and how we see each other, in this world in which we live.

As I compose this chapter, I am firstly going to concentrate on the word INTEGRITY!
Yes, I may have presented the title of this chapter, by having integrity as the first word.

However, I am of the belief, and disagree with me if you wish: This world in which you and I live and exist, deems, to some extent, that morals, (such as most of us define that word), are more important in their implication to human existence and honesty, than integrity.
We all have from time to time, conversations as regards moral issues.
It is usually a safe conversation, as regards other people and/or the country in which we live, because common courtesy keeps it in a very personal safe zone of conversation.
On the other hand, "integrity" is a totally different, very seldom, not discussed
Subject.
WHY? You might ask.
Because:
Morals, are virtually defined very clearly in the world's populations.
Integrity, is deemed to be a very personal way of one's way of living, and is regarded as a non-subject discussion topic.

Each and every one of us, on this planet of ours, has their own very clearly defined MODE OF INTEGRITY.

And, just as importantly, as we grow up, as we get older, as we age in years the level of integrity we determined, at some very definite time, (and place, in some instances), becomes an unchangeable integral part of us.

Also, at about this same time, morals and personal morality came into existence, to be part of a very personal, clear, understanding of oneself.

Know, that for most of us, this state of being, sort of came into mental existence, over time.

Then, as we aged, it became an integral part of our very personal integrity, set of morals and identity.

Sure, subject to changes from time to time, if we very personally decided this was to be so.

As I compose these few lines, I also know of, and will accept, that as this world moves into different phases of its existence in the universe, so will our personal integrity levels change.

Many years ago, mainly as part of my personal business vocation, I very personally, and totally committed, and determined, (now some forty plus years ago), that my level of integrity and morals, must and always will be beyond reproach.

I made this commitment to myself, to ensure in my mind, that my tax, accounting, and subsequent legal, attitudes to my practice, and its rules would remain morally unchanged. There would be no exception, and absolutely no excuses or justifications.

You may well ask, why promote myself so dramatically, at this time?

Initially, I intended that all chapters be in alphabetical sequence.

The fact that this has not eventuated, is pertinent to the nature of the topics, and further possible individualised discussion, outside of this publication.

My way of being, and attitudes to life and living, is no more or less important than yours, the reader.

I have also made the very clear choice, not to judge others by my own rules.

Each and every individual person, has their own, very personal, desirable, opinion on morality, and the knowledge of how it reflects on their personal way of being.

Conversations occur between family members, usually starting with stories about family members, and goes from there to the wider community.

Between neighbours, it is usually about their street, or the wider local community in which they live.

Then, the conversation develops to the wider community from there.

Between friends, it is usually about the city in which they live, the country in which they were born or lived, and eventually the conversation turns to the world in general itself.

Where do these discussions eventuate, or come from?
How do they eventuate on such a regular basis?
Why are morals so important, that this topic becomes the topic of conversation?

AND: have you noticed, when these conversations and discussions occur, there is invariably complete agreement!

This can not eventuate if INTREGITY is dragged into the conversation.

As stated previously, morals are a safe conversation. Integrity, is a very personal conversation, not for discussion.
And yet, both these issues are totally integral, to all living animals, fish, birds, and any other living beings such as ourselves, in this world in which we live.

It does not seem to matter, that the various participants or proponents of any/or the conversation, may have a single and/or many-sided personal opinions on morals and moral values. What does matter, is that invariably there is no discord in the group, and/or the discussion when it takes place.

This then raises the following supposition:
People who regard themselves as having a high level of integrity, (usually based on their very personal attitudes to life and living standards) or consider themselves basically honest, might discuss this subject of morals, in a context so totally different to that of a group of criminals.
But then, they may not!

Each of us, having reference only, to our own way of living, our lifestyle, our occupation, will have a personal preference point as to our input of views on morals, views that we usually or may promote, for discussion.
Views we may like aired to and with others!

It is not necessary here, to go into the many and various topics that could be covered by any discussion covering morals.

These may, or could be similar to items mentioned in other chapters and topics elsewhere in this book. Especially if some variation in presentation were to present itself.

BUT, good unbiased conversations with others, done in a friendly and compassionate way, are ALWAYS enjoyable, if no previously desired result is the end consequence.

I also believe that we might all agree, that the morals of our own and other societies, are made up of the differing values pertaining, to that country or locality in which the discussion takes place, or how the community in that place regards its personal moral values.

Then also, city dwellers are sure to have a different set of moral values as compared to those in a small town, village.

Farmers of remote rural areas, and/or farmers in general, may or might have totally divergent values and views, or possibly appear to city dwellers as being totally out of touch.

"Out of touch with what?" you may ask.

There would appear, to be no choice to be no conclusive answer, to that question!

There is another perspective to cover and consider.

This is in relation to our world's animal, bird and water kingdoms, its members, also ourselves, we being all the residents of this planet we call Earth.

Firstly, there those of us who have pets, be they cats, dogs, fish, birds, etc.

Where there are both sexes present, have you noticed that it is invariably the female of the species that determines the morality of that species.

In television presentations of lives of birds, frogs, fish, mammals, reptiles, insects and other living creatures, have you also noticed that is the female of those species that determines their moral values.

I am here, very definitely and specifically NOT referring to humanity.

Whilst I am totally aware, that there are always exceptions to any given statement, our knowledge of life and living in our human world, puts us as humanity, in a perspective, as being different from anything that is not a human animal.

A human being has the ability of choice!
The ability to choose, from right or wrong, good or bad, up or down, in or out, etc., so many other opportunities, all at the same, and/or one time, on a continuing, complex range of thoughts, all the time, at the same time, and at ANY time.

This choice ability, is not given to any other species that live or reside on earth.

Does this create the difference between humanity, and all other living things on earth.
Where there appears to be no choice, except for the choosing of a mate, and then I wonder, if in all and every case, this is correct, from my readings and TV shows.

Is this difference, subtly apparent to us all, in that there are no hard and fast rules covering the whole of humanity on mother earth?

Does this aspect of choice give humanity the choice to evolve, learn and experience living, in a subtly different way?
Do moral values become part of the things learnt from an early age?
Does this learning, from an early age, as we grow up, determine our morality, or our personal view of morality in later life?
Do our moral values change as we grow older?

So many questions, and apparently, not too many answers!

For each of us, it would subtly appear that it is much simpler to stick to vague discussions and assumptions, on moral values. This presumes, of course, that a specific topic or agenda was not set up at the commencement of any discussion.
I have no memory of being part of anything but general conversations, on the subject of morals.
I have NEVER, had a general discussion with others, with regard to integrity, as being the discussion item!

A question, "What are the life experiences that seem to be so different for each and every one of us, as human beings?

AND, I am asking again:
When discussion occurs on moral values, why is it that there is usually no aggression or discord between the participants in that discussion?

Why is it also so, that no concrete resolution appears, as a conclusive resolution to the discussion?
Are we, at those discussion times, being total in an honest conversation with other

We might then ask, "What is it that needs attention".

Are we really, as a society, in need of attending to any aspect, of that, which has an application to moral, or even, what may be termed, normal human values?

We all, that is all of us, would like to believe that the human body, and by association, our health vitality, and way of being, are working together, in order to give us all a form of morality, that could be called wellbeing.
And then, in all probability, all would be well with us.
There would be no concern, as about what other people were doing with their lives, in that, they were living, and being alive.

It is this aspect of not knowing, according to our own personal moral values, and integrity, that gives us this likely angst, and need for discussion.
But, only on moral topics.

Thus, are we doing "it" right?
Are we personally, in accord, with society, and its ever-changing values, concepts and precepts?

As each one of us is, individually different, there would appear to be a need to ascertain, that our personal differences can still be in "tune" with the "norm", whatever that normality appear to be, or to look like.

But this can only eventuate, or happen, from our own very personal normality, as we live our daily lives.

This would be a total acceptance of, our own very personal life principles.

The total principle of, "being in tune" with all those around us, even those we might meet occasionally, and/or, those we might come across, even if it is to be only once in a lifetime.

Personal principles, that appear to create a context, of how the rest of society, as we know and live in it, operates.

Thus, at some point in time, there will be conversations that will ensue.

Is it possible to discuss moral values and morality, in a general way?

Is it possible to not get specific at any time, during this discussion?

Is it, that in reality the opportunity to be specific, (integrity) is avoided, at all costs?

The reality is, that we as individual life form energies, have our own personal way of being human, and our own very personal set of moral values.

In presenting this point of view, it is most important to know, without any personal doubt, that in our own very personal way, we are on track, whatever that "track" may look like to yourself, and others.

Can we, or should we, afford ourselves, the personal privilege of standing up, and being counted, in the face of others, who not think in a manner the same as ourselves?

It is interesting to note that, the youth of the world could now enter the conundrum, where undoubted peer pressure comes into play.

Do adults also succumb to peer pressure, of a similar type, in perhaps a more subtle way?

What is the eventual possibility of a scenario, where all the members of the human race, from birth to death, will sing to the same tune as regards morality, in every one of all its forms and permutations.

As I compose this chapter, I am totally aware that different communities, and different countries, other than the one in which you and I reside, have differing moral values, and attitudes to those of myself.
These values and attitudes, most probably will be at variance to those I know and understand, and which I regarded as the norm.
This I completely understand.
That this world of ours, has so many variables, is something to be aware of, at all times.

The next chapters, I trust, I would also like to believe, will cover, maybe, some of the above and other life issues.

That, at this point, as part of all these writings, is what tolerance and integrity is all about, if nothing else is of importance.

"IN EVERY CHAPTER OF THIS WHOLE DOCUMENT".

That things, are not in accord with the way we, as individuals of different countries and regimes consider to be moral values, does not make them right or wrong.

They are just, the morality pertaining to that individual different culture, which has the right to believe it is its own form of perfection.

No more and no less.

AND, if it is not for you, the reader of this chapter, SO WHAT!

AS I compose the end of this chapter, I am totally aware that there is no "right" or "wrong" set of values for us to criticise, look at, discuss and/or evaluate.

But, it does raise the question of acceptance of the rights of others, to do their own thing, a right created by virtue of living in a different country, city, or community.

A right of being able, to live and breathe amongst others who might view life and living, from a perspective totally foreign to you the reader.

Tolerance, is the next chapter. What will it have to say and impart?

It is for you to decide.

Only you, no one else.

BUT: Let our statement on the next chapter be: TOLERANCE OF "ALL THINGS".

Tolerance

The word tolerance was used at the end of the previous chapter.

I believe, truly believe, I am a tolerant person.
But; maybe I'm not!

AND This chapter took a long, long, time to write.

Being as critical, to myself, as I could, or, believing I knew how, and on a very personal basis; alone, and with only my desk and computer, as company:
I self-criticized myself deeply, by the fact that I (as stated elsewhere) have
maintained that personal view, of always being totally honest, and being (at all times) totally aware of my vow of complete integrity to all, regardless!

Thus; I believe I am tolerant, as tolerant as it is possible to be, to all things, concepts, principles, ideas, and those whom I come into contact with, each and every day
As I live my life.
May we share some or all of these concept things together?

So!
What exactly is tolerance?
What is tolerance all about?
Is tolerance one thing or many things?

Is tolerance, as seen from a very individual personal perspective, a tolerance of all things?

I suspect not!

So, just as exactly as is possible by me, "THE QUESTION!"

WHAT DOES TOLERANCE LOOK LIKE?

Is it myself, maybe on my own, or maybe with other people?
Is it a small group of people talking?
Or maybe, it is a larger group of people?
Is it a community, a city, a nation, a religious gathering?

Is it also a reference point for those items, where we appear to have no say or control?
Those present-day things we see or view, people we meet, or possibly email, the App. on your phone, the internet, left waiting on a telephone call, a casual short conversation with someone, who takes too long to get to a point, subtle or otherwise.
Items, where we appear to have no say or control?
"I would like to think, I'm sure you've got the message."

THUS:
A personal, usually immediate, sense of evaluation and without a conclusion takes place on first meeting someone, possibly by invitation or pure chance.
Our own personal, unspoken, assessment (tolerance?), is immediately our first thought.

That is, when each of us, in say, possibly one of the scenarios presented above, becomes, and should/could be, a deciding factor in our own way, or mind, of what and how we communicate, what we will accept, offer or reject.

That also occurs when the person or thing, that is presented to us: is accepted, discussed, and/or rejected, either visually, verbally, or mentally.

On the mental side of those last couple of lines, it is marvellous as to how quickly we silently make up our minds, when unexpectedly we are introduced to a stranger.

We all, without exception, immediately form a personal very private opinion.
That opinion could be anything, looks, demeanour, speech, whatever.
Why do we do this?
Is this a subtle way of determining how tolerant we may want to be, in talking to, or relating to that person?

There is an old saying:
"Do not judge a book by its cover."

YET, there are very, very few of us who, DO NOT DO THIS, so called "book cover judging", over and over again, repeatedly.

We do this with respect to people, other living things, food, inanimate objects, just to pick on a few items.

Know that, I have not attempted here to define all the things we might judge in this manner.

And, know that I have made no attempt to cover the multitude of that which may be viewed, and/or looked over as regards, any level of possible tolerance and/or intolerance

As I write this, believe me, I know I am no different from you the reader.

I look at, or experience something, immediately forming, some sort of personal opinion, on and how it occurs to, and or, for me.

As children, we are exposed to the wishes of our parents. In that, more than mostly, our parents are both our teachers and instructors.

And, children are taught the tolerance or intolerance I am referring to, by well-meaning adults as part of their growing up experiences.

Most times, we adults refer to this tolerance concept, to our younger members of our community as "like or dislike".

At this point, some regard would need to be had, to include things outside of the personal requirements of family daily living, such as eating habits, common courtesies, wellbeing and health, not forgetting many other personal family etiquette type modalities.

On experiencing, almost anything, for the first time, we ALL immediately form an opinion: Like, dislike, tolerance, intolerance, whatever.

ALL human beings do this!

As we get older, towards adulthood, this like or dislike, becomes a form of tolerance, to take us all, into our older age or older life cycles.

All of us, being younger or older, perpetuate this thought pattern, developed as part of our learning experiences as children, into our adult living experiences.

Thus, within our previous childhood learning, we mentally or verbally react.
I could refer to this, as a "tolerance reaction".

This form of tolerance modality, may be almost immediate as a youngster, or may come later, or sometime later still, when one has taken the time, and sometimes also the effort, to think through their real or imagined like and dislike criteria.

Then, an opinion, on a personal level, of tolerance emerges.

Importantly, and usually for us all, as time and exposure progresses, we will just simply continue to have a like or a dislike.

That like or dislike, could also be accompanied by another different emotion or set of emotions, much more, say important than a like or dislike, but maybe on a level, way below intolerance, as and when the item or individual is in one's personal space or presence.

This then might be, if discussed with another, classified as a tolerance or intolerance, usually depending on the circumstances.

Each of us may at times, look closely at ourselves, in a personal effort to determine our ever-personal level of like, dislike, tolerance or intolerance.

However, as this tolerance concept usually has no bearing on daily living experiences, invariably it will get in the way of us considering to have enough time or energy, to do more than be tolerant, as and when meeting someone.

This may also relate to things, be they living or inanimate.

Then: is like or dislike of something, a measure of our tolerance?

When, we do at some point, a very immediate personal critical examination of another person or thing, one, some, or all of the following words may or could apply:

Beliefs	Insights
Inspiration	Philosophies
Dogma	Methodologies
Interaction	Sensing
Relationships	Emotions
Wounds or Scars	Insight

Please, do not think for a moment that this list is in any way complete.

It is but a reference only, to some of the various ways that each and every one of us may use our vital, personally inbuilt knowledge and abilities, to determine a choice of action, reaction, and/or maybe satisfaction.

Naturally, and at the same time, unless one wants to be needlessly rude, or impatient, there is little more said, but to make some lame excuse and move on quickly, if confronted by a chance unplanned meeting.

But then, is the above like or dislike of a thing, a measure of our tolerance?

In exactly the same measure as our like or dislike; is tolerance of a personal measure, of a person or their attitudes, something inanimate, or maybe something imagined?

Who knows?

In other words, as individuals, are we really tolerant.

Is our tolerance objective or subjective?

In this context:
To have something be objective is to have a realistic knowledge base, on which a considered valid opinion is made.
And, subjective becomes a means to determine an opinion based on nothing more than a maybe, a general and very personal like, dislike, or possibly aversion.

And in either case there is a bias, based on that predetermined and mentally known personal truly believed, life experiences and opinions.

With all of us, it does not matter that this personal opinion is not in context with other people, who may be with us at the time.

What we usually don't do, if in the presence of others, is blurt out our immediate opinion.

We usually listen, in what we think and believe, is a tolerant way, to what others are discussing.

At some point we may, or may not, enter the conversation with our own thoughts, usually on the basis of presenting a view that others will not think as being too opinionated.

Sometimes our tolerance of the conversation becomes too much to bear, and we have no regard for what other people think, before expressing our opinion.

Is this a form of intolerance?

And you could argue (maybe to the death of the discussion or argument) that your opinion is valid and will not change.

The reason you speak up in the first place.

It makes no difference in the scheme of things.

Your likes and or dislikes might be a form of tolerance or intolerance.

Just be aware – that's all.

CHANGING YOUR WORLD

Think back,

If you are an older adult – say, 30, 40,50 years ago. Maybe longer still, if you desire, as and when you read on.

For the younger generations, from say from age 15 to 30.

And everyone else, it's up to you!

But, for the younger generations reading this, see if you can sit with someone older, if they will let you, and I trust they will!

Now, I would ask you to go back to the earliest memories of your life.

The older years you are content, only go that far, or wherever you care to go back to.

For myself, as one of my clear memories, our public school (now known as primary school) and the schoolroom which had huge windows, no heating and no lighting, shared wooden desks with inkwells(empty), and a teacher who was deadly with small pieces of chalk, if he felt you were misbehaving. He would throw them at you with deadly accuracy.

Then you had to take them back to him, and apologise.

Those memories don't hurt me, 'cos, in those days, were part of the deal.

At the same time, now have no relevance to the school classrooms of today.

So, maybe I give my age away somewhat.

But, why do I remember this so clearly?

The scenario, or living experience if you want it thus, has to my inquiring mind, no valid reason for its continuing memory!

But, it was possibly, in my much later working years, a memory that became important in the need to concentrate on learning, to achieve the desired results in my professional career.

The reason I bring it up is, that too often in life events take place that appear to be unimportant at the time, but have a bearing on later living.

It is also important to stress here, that there are some activities or events, that at best, become forgotten memories.

The biblical words; "Get ye behind me Satan" when said or thought with meaning and intention, is but one way (without having a religious aspect) of moving on to the next, intended project, or way of being.

To the present:

I continuously look at my life now, with its computers, I Pads, I Phones, tablets, mobile telephones, Foxtel, (still have a stereo), and so many other new devices, all that are way ahead of my memory of Dick Tracy's wrist watch in the comic books, and, you don't see comic books any more either.

And, as I mention these things, I am continuously aware of the fact that we should not leave out things like solar energy, satellites, medical advances, etc.

And, I realize and know my world has changed dramatically in my lifetime, and will continue to change as a result of our technological knowledge basis, on life and living on mother Earth.

But this chapter is not about these or those sorts of changes – it is about the title of this book, the way we are.

To venture into this chapter, is akin to taking a great leap of faith in the direction in which humanity is moving on an almost daily basis.

I am reminded, as I write this chapter, of a saying I grew up with:

"Things were better in the old days."

I am quite happy to accept that "things" in the old days were different- but "better" – I think not.

If you have read; "How do we show up in Life", (Chapter 2) you will recall some lines on the word, "better", on the 1st page and a few pages later.
As I said there, the word "better" has different meanings to different people, very much depending on that person's personal point or points of view, and where they are in their own personal life.

This chapter is about "YOU".
"You", changing your world.

And, you can and could change your world, in any way you want. In any way, shape or fashion.
You, the individual reading this chapter.

I readily agree that each of you may, or do have, that personal right and choice, but at the same time, may also be very content with the way things are in your life, at this point in time.

And, as I write this, I also realize there will be some who have no intention of changing their world.
They are content the way things are.

That I might include myself in this category, is not what I am discussing here.

I appear to have digressed somewhat, but this is intentional.

At the start of this chapter I indicated some things that have changed our world, just in our lifetime, and changes that will continue to occur in all aspects of technology, and subsequently in the living of our daily lives.

The "changing your world" I am referring to, is with regard to your personal self.
Your way of being, your responses to life and living, your method of relating to others and how others relate, or may relate to you.

Thus, is it necessary or appropriate that you consider changing your world?
Only YOU, the reader, are **entitled** to make that decision.

On your own personal basis, you can change your world in many different ways – such as – changing your house, your car, your relationship or relationships, your diet, or doing something else that I have not mentioned, but which is more or less specifically appropriate for you.

In some respects, doing any one or even all, of the above mentioned things, is not changing your world.
Because your world is YOU!

SO! Just what am I getting at?

As we live our lives, we become an integral, very personal, part of our own very intricate personality, and this, our daily living experiences.
That is to say, each and every human being living on the world of ours, which some call "Mother Earth", are in fact continuing to do those things that are comfortable and realistic, given that which all of us have spent many years creating.

Change for change's sake most often does not appear to many of us to be an option we are prepared to contemplate.

We all, from time to time, look at other people doing their own thing, and think to ourselves, "We could do that."
But invariably we just don't.
Not because we can't, but because other things in our lives seem or appear, to be more important than the possibility of being, shall we say, "outrageous", going off in what might be looked at, by others, as an unpredictable and virtually unknown tangent.
A tangent that others, who know and understand us, yes, and love us in their own familiar way, might question.

Those who are prepared to change their world are few and far between, and most times are regarded by others as someone to be careful of, when we are around them.

Be totally aware that:
Humanity, and the culture of ALL countries, values stability in ALL things, ALL the time.

To be viewed as different, all of a sudden, in some manner or other, becomes a challenge to many people as they look on to just what you are getting up to.
Mostly, this is about, not trusting a possibly different personality, emerging all of a sudden.

BUT: For some of us, an event occurs, which on the very personal face of it, creates a dramatic change in our way of being, and possible ultimate living concepts and ideals.

That individual has, to some of us, become someone different.
They have, in being different, changed their world.
This is the sort of change I am referring to in this chapter.

Always remember, and also know.
No one person in the world, will ever be the same as any other living person.

It may appear, to any one of us, and at a very personal level, that change is deemed appropriate or necessary.

Only you, can be the judge of that decision.
And only you, can determine in your own way, how, or when, that change will eventuate.

It may be a decision that other people will notice.

It may be a decision that no one else will, or be required to notice.

It may be a decision to tell no one, and see who might be inquisitive enough to ask, "what is happening?"

It is important to mention here, that the younger generations of this world of ours are, almost in a continual mode of change. Think about what these younger generations, are doing with their lives as you read this chapter.

I have previously mentioned technology, as a component of change.

A component of current living, so different to our and/or the older generations.

The almost unbelievable changes that are occurring to our world as I write this, might possibly have some of us asking ourselves, how do we keep up?

I have presented this as a question. But, is it really a question? I would suggest, more like a question, that has no immediate logical answer.

But/or, do we want to keep up with change and technologies and its influence on our lives into the future?

This chapter is not about these things either.

It is about your own very personal decision to change something, or nothing.

A decision to change nothing might be the most appropriate thing to do.

And yet, there might be that niggling feeling, somewhat later in life.

"What If?"

I wish you well in your decision.

Pets In Our Lives

Some people have no pets.
Some people have one pet.
Some people have many pets
Some people have different kinds of pets.
Some people keep animals, birds, amphibians, snakes, or some other kind of species. They might not be regarded as pets, but in some sort of reality, are their pets that they care for.

And my wife and I have two mutts, (dogs to you) and two moggies, (they are cats), who are in our care, as our pets.

Therein may be a question:
Do the spiders with their webs on the walls, which we don't feed, sort of tolerate, and mostly ignore, fall into the pet category?
As well as those birds, that breed in the garage ceiling every spring, and leave heaven knows what there, when the chicks and themselves depart.
More or less pets?
Just a thought!

And, is Leo one of our cats, currently helping me type this by sitting on my arm, purring contentedly at the moment, possibly our special cat?

Well maybe he is, because he has the loudest purr, of the two cats.

I cannot leave either or both dogs out of this conversation, because they, with one continually wagging tail, (Jessee was born without a tail), lots of mannerisms, like following me wherever I go, or their thanks too I suppose, or maybe trust and love, and food, and attention for including at times, the small food tid bits.

Is this all it takes to keep them happy and contented?
Are my wife and I the only people content to nurture, or care for, our pets?
I think not!

We are both aware, through the likes of news and TV reports, of what happens to some unwanted animals, such as those that become bait.
Things that you and I cringe too, when we hear what has been done to some defenseless animal.

Enough; I am talking about, "pets **in** our lives,"

Those, who have no pets, would be able to give a valid reason of why this is so.
The reason matters not, rather than raise the question.
I believe, there will always be that personal, valid reason.
And, that person, or maybe family reasoning, is to them, just as valid as my own excuse, for always having a dog near me continually.

There is a small exception to that last statement!

As a younger person, and as mentioned elsewhere in this series of chapters.

Possession of pets was an almost non event, except as defined elsewhere.

I seem to have concentrated to this point, only on cats and dogs.

But on two occasions, for my wife and I, there have been birds too, all of whom were/are Australian Parrots.

Firstly, a Sulphur Crested Cockatoo.

This bird is purely Australian, but is bred for overseas markets.

A pure white bird with a brilliant yellow crest.

Usually noisy, but this breed can be taught to speak audibly.

Can be handled, but capable of a nasty bite, if mishandled.

Later on, A pair of King Parrots. Slightly smaller than the Sulphur Crested.

This parrot has a chest that is bright red, a breast and crest a blue front turning to a bright green at the tail feathers.

Mainly a bush parrot, relatively scarce, living naturally, in Australian dense bush mountainous areas.

I am not aware of any ability to speak, but, beautiful to look at, and not readily a bird to handle.

A government permit is a requirement to own and look after these King Parrots.

For those not living in Australia, may I suggest you look them up on Google or Wikipedia. The colours are vividly dramatic.

Now, as a definite aside, I have given you my birth country, just above: AND
I was born in Sydney, and have lived in Victoria since I left the Navy in 1962
Both, in the local state city, Sydney and Melbourne.

Back to the topic:

I appreciate that this, my point of view, on animals (and the birds) may be because these are the only pets I have ever had in my lifetime.
And the fact, that in their own way there is ongoing recognition of the love and care my wife and I, firstly, gave to the birds, and continually to the many cats and dogs, those we have had, and continue to have, and with those who are still with us.

But, there are so many other creatures out there, who are showered with love and respect by their owners.
Guinea Pigs, rabbits, fish, mice or rats, snakes, different kinds of cockatoos, terrapins, tortoises, just to name a few.

So, the question comes to mind.
What is it about we humans, that people, do continue to have pets in their lives?
Pets that have to be cared for in some way and/or fashion.
And that! No pets, after a lifetime of having them around me, does not appeal as an option!

Which, now takes me to the aspect of the love and attention my/our pets return to us, "At All times".

Love and attention, that has no guile, questioning, (except at meal times, when it doesn't happen soon enough for them), or apparent regard for anything, but total affection and total loyalty.

As I compose this missive, there are many cultures, that have those, that we call pets, as a food source.
Be that as it may! Culture is what it is, in some countries.

This chapter is about pets, in our lives

Pets, that we wish to look after.
And, in return, who in their own way, know we are looking after them.
And, return that love, in their own manner and way.
Let us also not ignore special assistance dogs, who are able to see, smell, hear, and other abilities, to assist so many people throughout this world of ours.

And, those specially trained dogs, who assist in the detection of illegal imports, into the various ports of most countries in this world of ours.

I am sure, we are all aware, that there are animals that, because of their specific training are able to do tricks.
Personally, as I see and watch these activities, I am also very aware of the bond between the animal and their trainer.

And, there are also those who train animals, capable of manifesting control over, whom I call "the ungodly", in our society.
I also note the positive affection between that animal, and the handler.

You might now ask?

What do I get out of, having a pet?

I can only but answer for myself and my wife:

It is, amongst other things: The gentle nudging, when either of the dogs want to share, what looks interesting, and may taste good.

Either one, or both of us, as part of the sharing and having something, food mostly, with them.

The continually tail wagging, dogs do when they are contented.

Their continuous barking, at the front door, as we get home in the car, eventually opening that door, no matter how or long or short a time we've been absent.

Yes, our dogs live in our house, with us, and the cats too.

Not only that, but they live together, in peace and harmony the whole time.

A resounding YES: It is possible.

Their purring, the cats that is, as you scratch or rub them.

I've mentioned Leo previously, Sox getting warm, in front of the heater, and rousing himself for some attention and a scratch, the occasional meow, to ask for more one on one.

And at the same time, the dogs who are lying alongside the cats, wanting their own little bit of attention, at the same time.

These animals, and previously the birds, are my own and my wife's love rewards!

What are yours?

Knowing

Each and every one of us, has a real knowing about something special, and at the same time, a knowing about many other things.

Thus, the art of knowing may or could be considered as a learning ability.

And, this knowing, which is often referred to as knowledge, would have been learnt in some way or fashion, from your birth.

As you read this chapter, you are, let's say standing, in your current world of being alive, receiving income of some sort, from wherever, and in an abstract way, learning more, to add to your knowing.

For each and every one of us, there comes a time in our lives, where we all, sort of believe, we know enough.

Before I go on, I would like to set a scene for those who believe they know.

There are certain organisations, that knock on your front door, because they wish to impart their knowing.

Most times it is of a religious nature, of the individual's practicing faith and beliefs in life and living.

Most likely, all of us at some time, have had some sort of contact with these well-meaning individuals.

I use the above scenario as a means of imparting to you, my reader, an ability that that is available to us all.

Bur referring to my first paragraph wherein I stated that my belief:
"Knowing is a learnt ability".

I believe, that we as humanity are all totally aware of many religions and cults. And, where there is no way, you or I are going to change the attitude of the individuals, who present themselves or their beliefs to us.

As I present the previous paragraph, please believe, I am in no way disparaging of you, the reader, and/or your cultural or religious beliefs.

That which you believe, is going to always be: "Your Knowing

I have my own very personal knowing, that it is not my privilege, to decide another person's beliefs are anything more or less than the integrity of exactly how they present themselves to the world.

As another example to us all; how many times have you been at a party, social gathering, BBQ, or whatever.
You are lined up, say getting your meal, and someone, male or female, waiting nearby, will insist their point of view is the only point of view that has any sort of integrity or honesty.

Personally, in both of the above situations, I listen as politely as possible, often presenting in as polite a way as possible, my own probable opposing contradictory point of view, and escape as soon as is possible.

Most times, this possible tirade on our mental abilities, happens when we are not in the frame of mind to react in a way that gives positive possible alternatives.

And here, you may ask, what is a positive way?

I could answer: "That to know is to be positive", but that answer does not define just what "knowing" is.

To go back to the above confronting circumstances, created by individuality,
I would also like to include, an event, or happening, as possibly being just as confronting.

May I suggest that as a species, humanity is usually composed of polite, informed and caring individuals.
We allow others to have their personal point of view, as long as those points of view, does not intrude on our own personal space or existence.

And yet, in the preceding chapters I have presented to you, the reader, "The Way-We are" as a possible way of being.
AM I, in some form or another, presenting to you my own knowing?
I trust not!
And yet I know I am!

Where to from here I now ask myself.
And, where to, from here, for you, the reader?

I now ask you: Is the knowing I am presenting not only in this chapter, but in this total document, but a way of looking at life and living?

And why, at this point in time, in the book you are reading?"

What I know, is exactly that: what I know.

And you, the reader in your own lives have your own knowing, whatever that may be.

Your own very personal way of life and living that is or has been determined by your own very personal knowing of the way things are learnt and done.

There is no right or wrong, just knowing.

In previous chapters I have stated that: "You are OKAY the way you are."

This is a variation on the title of this book. But, it is now specifically given to you, the reader, to determine your own life and learning as you live that life, which makes you the individual you are.

At this point in the narrative I would like to present you with a saying I usually keep to myself, a saying I picked up from somewhere many years ago.

You do not get to vote on the way it is.
You already did!

To me this represents my attitude to my present life,
or,
I am who I am.

I created my life, my lifestyle, the person I am, that which I live by, the knowledge I have, the knowing I know,
and,
most times, I am content.

Business As Usual

You might well ask "What do I mean – Business as Usual"?

Many years ago, I attended a seminar lasting some four days. This term, business as usual, continued to come up in the conversations.
Deliberately, by the seminar leader.
For me, the term eventually meant: "We are who we are"/"It is what it is"

Over the years, I have attended many seminars.
Self-improvement, Organisation, Dealing with crisis, Management, Self-ownership, Time management, to name most of them.

I would leave these seminars, full of ideas and concepts. Such as:
I am definitely going to do this or that - whatever!
This time I will be different, and make a difference!
I will make a change on how I present myself, and how I will present my work space.
How I can create valid organisation, in my daily work schedule!
Keep, and continue keeping a work diary!
Create a schedule for remembering appointments!
And a few more I cannot recall.

These concepts are, or were, a part of my working day, my recreation, my hobbies and/or my general activities, but mainly aimed at my business potentialities to be, even more successful.

Looked at in another way – each motivational seminar I have attended, or been part of, has promised, my world will change if I follow the various presenters' guidelines.

Just as an aside, I might somewhere have a discussion on the true meaning of the word, "promise" or "promises" as such.
And, if I don't.
The word "promise" means nothing.
As we live our lives, that word ceases to exist.

However, on with business as usual.

It was also invariably stated that, work, life, and living, after the seminar, will be more enjoyable, relationships with your partner and others will improve, things of immediate importance will be immediately attended to – rather than left on the back burner.
And so on.

No matter how enthusiastic I might have been, about changing an aspect of my attitudes, at the end of a particular seminar or event, the effort I subsequently put in to be different, or maybe present myself differently to others – in the long term - nothing ultimately changed much – if at all.

I now realise, that as I have grown older, my attitude to life, living, work, and other things has matured somewhat, and changed.

And as I consider the word changed in composing the previous sentence, I am in fact, now living a different business as usual.

Or, to put it in a different context, my now different "business as usual", as I have grown older, and retired from business earning activities, relates to age.

So, I have now, in a totally different way, created a totally different "business as usual" way of being.

My wife tells me, this is maturity!

My wife will also tell you; I am not the same person I was, all those years ago, and, many years previously.

But, my knowing of my personal self tells me that, inwardly I believe I am the same person I always was.

And yet, I know I'm not, but in my own mind I believe, I am just a little older and still, sure to a lesser extent, doing the things I always did, in the same way and manner, that continually took place those many years ago.

So, for me, is it still business as usual, using the knowledge and ability, gained over many previous years of knowing how?

Or, the creation of a variation to business as usual?

Or, a totally new creation of a totally different form of "Business as Usual", to take me into my future years.

My years ahead, still to come as an older male, but with a non-existing concept.

So, it's a totally different "Business as Usual" concept, that my mind has yet to come to grips with.

Those who know and understand me, tell me I have a softer personality now, compared to how I was, some years back.
I leave you, the reader, to interpret the word "softer".
For me however, as regards my inner self, it is still "Business as Usual"
My personality is the same, I still maintain my sense of integrity built up over many years.
I believe I still treat those whom I meet, in the same manner I have always done.

So, have I altered my attitude to life and living and those to whom I relate?
Or, at the same time, know I am still the same person I've always been.

You, the reader, might well ask, at this point in the narrative, "Where is this conversation going?"

Let me continue.

I mentioned elsewhere, an old Chinese philosophy that determines our lives and living and is based on 3 x 7 year cycles.
Go back to the chapter – INTERLUDE (page 61), if you wish.

One Christian church says "Give me a child till when he is 7, and he is mine for life – and then, do with him that which you will".

I believe this, to be a different aspect of the same philosophy. Most probably there are other philosophies also echoing the same concept.

In presenting this aspect of life and living to my clients, friends and others, a realisation usually becomes apparent with themselves, and those that they have known, or know, there is some truth in the concept.

So – where to from here?

Back to the name of this chapter - "Business as Usual"

At this point – before you read any further – I am requesting you to sit quietly.
Now, think back into your past, and bring back to your mind memories.
You may also consider, to write down some of those memories, as you: –
Firstly – think back to your childhood – say to age 10 – and rediscover some memories of your life at that time. Good and/or bad things – it really doesn't matter.
As you recall the memory, or memories of your life at that time, ponder on your current way of being, to yourself, to your relatives, to the community and especially to your attitude to life.

For some of you it will be appropriate or necessary to ignore the current technical age we have become accustomed to. Go right back to the very basic you, your true inner self.

I believe you will basically find that you are now, who you were then, as regards your personality and regard for life and living.

There is a little room below to write some personal thoughts in your own hand if you wish, or perhaps, use a separate page to compose and/or create some very personal thoughts.

Did you write a brief two or three words on what enthused you? And then a very short observation on why nothing changed. Or

Maybe what happened to make a difference in your life. Or

Has nothing changed – You are who you are.

"I wonder,"

Choices – One or Many?

First, one thing – then another – then another ---

What might this mean to you?
Is there a desire to understand the meaning or even meanings of the two words, either as separate or combined type thinking tools, available to everyone? THUS:

Each day, as we all go through our day's activities, things occur.
They may be expected or planned.
But, very often and/or often as not, the planned day doesn't sort of work out as was intended.

On a personal level, I am an early riser, mostly to get the previously planned activities completed, before the more than probable interruption occurs.
As part of my professional career, (as a CPA), this quiet time is invariably used as an important time to resolve issues, that are most times, specifically related to a client related conceptual and/or taxation problem.

For me, the energy of the pre-dawn quiet and serenity, I regard having a precious energy.

But, the telephone rings, my commitment to job no. 1 is in jeopardy, as I answer that call.

No, it is not in business hours, and I know clients are totally aware of how I work. And, they also know I always seem to be available.

AND: IT IS NOT A MOBILE PHONE. Not quite that monster, **but** an interruption nonetheless.

BUT: My successful accounting practice is based on the premise of always being available.

Thus, my CHOICE in this specific instance is: TO BE AVAILABLE.

Why do this to yourself? – you may ask:

At this point in these writings, I could spend time giving an explanation, but that will only justify to me, reasoning I made some 40 plus years ago.

I will comment that this choice was a reason for being in business. And, it was a great choice! And, it worked!

Choices, for each person are based somewhat on personal, work, recreational, travel, and so many other personal values, that make up the life of each and every other individual person, on Mother Earth.

There is very definitely, "NO one size fits all" in respect of life and living choices.

Within the context of this chapter on choice, is the scenario of the ways and methods, of and in our lives.

The way and methods we use as we very personally live that life, and how the many choices made on a day to day basis, seem in some way to come together.

There is a very old saying, I recall my mother often giving me. Many more years ago than I care to remember:

"THE ROAD TO HELL IS PAVED WITH GOOD INTENTIONS"

At the time, and many years into and to my present age; It meant as explained by mum; choose carefully and wisely if you can, because you will have to live with the result.

A request:

Put this chapter aside for a few moments, sit quietly on your own, with maybe a cuppa in front of you, or in your hand, specially if it is a cold and/or rainy day, "Just what am I writing about, from your personal perspective?"

Obviously, it's about choices. Grab a pen and paper if you wish! Ascertain the good ones firstly, just a few words from your memories!

Call to mind some bad or lousy ones, especially those you never were going to talk about again! – Remember, there is no talking, so you can do this!

Recall also, the irrelevant, the impulsive, the stupid, family events, whatever.

Back to the statement on the previous page.

In my very early years, when I now sort of remember hearing those words, from mother, and also from time to time from other family members, I did not really understand just what "hell" was. I knew however it must have been something bad.

Time moves on, and understanding, thankfully comes into play, on life and living.

I have not digressed, to my mind, from the title of this chapter. What I am driving at, is, that as, a child, the words choice or choose, were never (as far as I remember) given me as an option, on what to do next, as and when childish decisions had to be made.

Achieve exactly, that which you intended and/or planned? NOW!

A project to work on. It could be just for yourself, OR involve others, if you wish.

Arm yourself with a pen, and paper to write on.

Something appropriate to include amongst these pages. I make this suggestion as your writings may be very personal, and are NOT for others.

Any answers are personal.

There is no right, no wrong, just comments and/or answers. Perhaps also, copy these questions on to a separate piece of paper, to file with your answers.

Pick a subject or activity you clearly remember, from some choice activity you recall from the past.

1. Did you Achieve exactly, that which you intended and/or planned?

2. Did you Achieve sufficiently, to justify (**only to yourself**), a result that gave you personal satisfaction?

3. Did you find in the process, a personal sense o satisfaction, or satisfying achievement?

4. Were other thoughts occurring to you, on other things that may or might have been included in the project and/or activity?

5. Is it more than possible that there may have been (at the time), other things to consider, as part of that project?

6. Did you achieve whatever there was to achieve, relative to the end of the project?

7. Is the project ongoing – that is – is it a sort of lifetime way of knowing and or learning?

8. Is it, or was it, a sole personal project. Based on that which you wished to achieve – and that which you did, or have to date achieved?

9. Was it that this personal project, may have involved others, in order to achieve a resolution?

Coming out of these questions, are other aspects of our lives and living requirements.

Like, do we have a real choice in what is next in our lives, or maybe something new comes into our lives, possibly taking it up as it could be likened to be something wild and exciting.

THUS:

Do you have a choice?

Are you able to make a clear and precise choice on the next step you may, or might take?

How do you request assistance, to assist or help you, on that next choice?

If you had no choice, what do you do?

At the end of what you believe to be a successful project, what do you do?

AND, so many questions, with no immediate answers, that occur on an almost daily life of living!

What I believe is important to me, and I trust to you too, you the person reading this chapter, is the fact that, as long as one maintains to others, their own personal level of integrity, under **all** circumstances, all will be "well".

To conclude:
Each and every person in this world of ours has an EGO, which creates our own choices, and then prompts us, in whichever way, to promote those our own successes.

This is, in the context of this discussion, a good thing.

There is another very old saying:
"Don't hide your light under a bushel".

But, in choosing to voice your personal success to others, "BEWARE".
This world of ours, is full of jealous people!

The belief you have in your success, or successes, is composed of your personal ability to know your true self.

Each and every one of us, makes the choice to determine our own valuation of how successful we are.
Yes, we invariably choose to evaluate success in comparison to something else.
The people I am referring to here, may be friends, relatives, acquaintances, or any person you meet casually.

You may not personally agree with me, when I say, thank goodness we are ALL, every one of us, different
Seeing things from differing perspectives, even noticing the difference. To those of our own personal life choices.

Choice again:

Your choice to disclose to others, that which you are still working on.

And, as the days pass into weeks, or even years, your life choices, changes of direction, may end up in a discussion of, "how you could have done better.

I am reminded of a previous chapter, as I make use of the word "better".

Its use is usually used in a form of subjective discourse, and always has manifold meanings.

As you go through life, you understand, or get to know, that choice is going to be very much part of your life.

Do not, give yourself a hard time over your life choices.

Put in another way, your choices in your life, and your living aspects.

Those choices, your personal life choices, such as where you live, learn and love, are those which occur at your own, very personal pace.

By all means, look for more things to do.

And, at the same time, be serene and content, with that which you are currently doing.

THIS IS!
YOUR CHOICE!
ONE OR MANY!

Opportunity Satisfaction Ego

It is possible, that in previous chapters, I might have, in a very indirect way, presented information that you might regard as some form of opportunity.

But then, you would be entitled to say that you had been reading concepts that you already knew of and about.

So then, just what could opportunity be, or what might opportunity look like?
AND: Is there a sense of satisfaction, coming out of ANY opportunity?

I do believe that, only you will be in a position to think, and make different decisions, referencing those question,
And only you, will be able to give yourself an honest answer.

I make these comments on the basis that, all human beings look at life and living, in respect of the "I", in our presentation of ourselves, that is, the I or ME, to the rest of the world.

Another way of presenting the previous paragraph is, "Looking Good".
Looking good is also about ego, and without EGO, I believe, the human race, would not be in existence!

The "ego" of each and every human being, is very personal.

Each and every single human being. THAT IS – EACH AND EVERY PERSON IN THIS WORLD OF OURS, has their own very personal identity, of which ego is a part.

My English Penguin Dictionary (1981 edition), in part states: an individual's experience or conception of himself, the self in contrast with outer objects, being true reality.
Our very personal EGO is, what drives us all continually:
To be alive.
To create, and in that creation process, is an aspect of perfection, as an opportunity.

I now ask, at this conjuncture, "What is opportunity anyway?"

To repeat myself somewhat, a possible, more plausible thing to say, or could be; Each and every one of us is, very much into, "Looking Good" (whatever that may mean to you, on a very personal basis).

And, each and every human being, continues to create, a personal life environment, by looking for some form, or style, or opportunity, a satisfying end result, or even, abstract completion.

Then, is it possible that, some of the statements above, or all of them, may lead to further very personal opportunities?

And, thereby our own very personal ego, is the main factor, that drives each and every one of us, to create, our own form of opportunity, completion and satisfaction.

Is opportunity, in some form or other, available to us all?

This answer is a definitive, YES!

And satisfaction?
Therein, lies a conundrum!

I have yet to meet the individual who can say they are totally satisfied, or, even satisfied.
It matters not which area of satisfaction is hinted at, or discussed.

In life and living, as we all partake of our daily activities, (such as they are, or might be), there will always be that item or activity still incomplete.

With regard to my own personal life and living activities, there are things to attend to on a daily basis, things that can wait, and those items which are awaiting my attention.
I am more than certain, that as you read the above statement, your own daily living activities will be, sort of identical.

Thus, on occasion I am satisfied with what has been attended to during the day.
Did it get to completion?
Sometimes yes. Sometimes no.

Can I, or should I be satisfied, with regard to that which I attended to, during the day?
Yes, if I leave my personal ego out of the thinking process!

If, and when I might add that word EGO, into the mental conversation, I am forcing my "personal ego" into the thinking process, which will automatically mentally tell ME, I could have achieved more.

In actual fact, there is no option, but to personally acknowledge some sort of inadequacy in my personal ability to be my word, on a day to day basis.

Sorry about that. Much as I would like to be perfect; it ain't going to happen.

I personally, on occasion, am "totally satisfied" with what I have achieved, completed or finalised.

But, this has always been on the basis of a singular item and/or project.

If and when, I add the actual word EGO into the equation, I do not believe I would be in any position, to come close to a "yes" answer.

Humanity, all of humanity, is continually searching for some ultimate form of completion or finalisation.

In the history of the world, this has never eventuated.

How many times, has the world announced, "We have the answer."

And, some time later, a discovery occurs, one that makes that previous answer, somewhat incorrect.

As I write this, I recall the introduction of the "Apple" computer, it was the "Ants Pants" to coin a phrase, or, the first mobile phone. (Brick to some), which for its initial size, is now so totally obsolete.

I do not believe I have roamed, away from the title of this chapter.

OPPORTUNITY AND SATISFACTION

And, you might think I missed the full stop, on the line above, after the word satisfaction. I DIDN'T.

Our world is creating an infinite number of opportunities at this present time.

This chapter is not about, the why of this taking place.

It, our human world that is, is also aimed at the satisfaction level of just what is, "taking place."

And, as I see or note these transitions; taking place almost daily?

YES! A question mark!

I do not dare go any further, there would appear to be no answer, specific or not.

Our world is **not** about technology!

It is about **US, HUMANITY**!

It is my belief, that as we gain the opportunities to fulfill our life and living experiences, and also the way this occurs, we move in a direction that gives us the opportunity to give some thought to, and maybe do something different.

Whatever that may be.

Or, we believe and know, we are content with our life experiences, as they have evolved to date.

And, at the least, we present ourselves to others, in a way that we are content in our understanding, of our current set of circumstances.

Could this attitude, be a form of perfection?

The answer (I suppose) could be a YES!
In a very individual way, that any one, or many of you reading this chapter, accept as potentially, perpetual perfection or satisfaction, as part of life and being alive.

SO, just where does opportunity, satisfaction, and then, a possible form of personal
perfection, come together in our life and our "living" lives.
Or, is it only appropriate and necessary to obtain our own personal view of things in our life and "living" personal arena.

THIS, then maybe leaves us with the CHOICE we have made in our lives, to be tolerant, of our own learning and experiences.

I have very deliberately introduced, (in capitals) the word CHOICE, into this narrative.
I have done this because ultimately, everything we do in our lives, comes down to choice.

Could it be, then, that Opportunity and Satisfaction, gets down to nothing more than CHOICE?

The right and privilege, to choose!
The decision, to make a choice!
And the ultimate prize:

The choice made, allows and gets one to create the opportunity.

At this point in the narrative, I would ask you to consider again the word "CHOICE."

Throughout the narratives in the previous chapters, I may have used this specific word, CHOICE, to define the "who you are", or even, "who are you" in order to make some definition, of the type of person you are.

Each of us, in our various ways of living, and being alive, are and will be, exactly who we want to be.

You, may be contemplating a very concise attitude as regards the previous statement.

I maintain; however, we choose. And, if you do not like the word, choice?
What other word would you specifically use or name, to define your current attitude and position in your own, very personal life?
It's your choice, to make the particular reason for your own set of circumstances.

Sure, there are public rules and regulations, we believe we must adhere to, in living in the community of which we are a part.

But, at the same time, I believe we will all be aware of those, who have made the choice, maybe to move to their own place of isolation, or heaven, or whatever.

And maybe, in so doing, creating for them, what they believe to be their own personal life opportunities.

We, you and I, will never know if satisfaction was also created as well!

If we ask ourselves, that very personal satisfaction question, would we genuinely get an answer, one that might or could satisfy the reason we asked the question, in the first place?

Each and every, single one of us, without exception, chooses a way, or more specifically, our way of being.

Chooses opportunity or opportunities.
Chooses a personal, level or levels of satisfaction.

That word, CHOICE, appears, again!

MEDITATION

Continually, as we learn new and/or different aspects of living and learning, and more especially as could possibly be related to the various chapters in this book, I have on occasion, in attending a seminar or two, which can remain nameless at this time, been informed that it will be necessary to meditate.

The word, "meditate" to me in my earliest of days, meant nothing more than to take one's mind into a sort of arena, one that meant, somehow to stop thinking.

It would appear, now thinking back to those times, that it was expected without any form of explanation, one had a knowledge of meditation, how to do it, and I now presume, to expect some sort of – I still don't know what, when or how!

Back to my dictionary, again:
Meditate: think deeply, repress normal mental activity so as to gain spiritual insight; muse; ponder; plan; intend.
Pity I didn't look up the meanings, many years before now.

Much later, many years later in fact, I was attending a 10-day seminar in the USA, where that word, meditation came up again.
This seminar was about: The "being" of Human Being.
Someone then made the comment I remember well: I don't know to meditate and how is it done?

As it was explained at the time, and as I recall!

Sit quietly, and as comfortably as you can.

There are other people in the room, making their own noises. There will be things going on outside of this room, ignore them, they are none of your business.

Initiates in occult practices, take many, many months, or years, to begin to learn how to meditate, in silence, and without the requirement of intrusion in unwanted thoughts. Know and accept this.

As you sit quietly, your active mind will, without any assistance from you, bring up something having nothing to do with you sitting quietly.

Accept this thought, and immediately let it go!

Another thought will almost immediately drop in: accept it too, and immediately let it go.

Do this as many times as it occurs.

At some point, your subconscious mind will attempt to still unwanted thought activity, or lessen the impact on your active mind.

That is the time, to tune into the particular modality as designated for this meditation session.

Have it be; the predominant issue; ignore other thoughts, as far as you can.

It does work, after some years of practice.

AND, as an example, and as I create topics for this series of chapters, I focus my mind on that which I believe is going to be the next appropriate comment, for that chapter.

But, occasionally, what do I believe to be the next, or an additional chapter heading?

I do not go anywhere near thinking about, what will be in that chapter.

That is for when I finish typing the heading.

I do trust this short explanation will assist you in your proposed or next attempt at meditation, and then, into the future.

Thoughts & Thinking

In a previous chapter, the one on meditation, reference was made to the very natural human virtue, of ever continuing thoughts, coming into existence as we go through our days' activities.

It occurred to me that I had treated this aspect of human nature, or way of being human, as something we all, take for the way things are.

That is, specifically with regard to this topic, thoughts and the human thinking process, I am very inclined to believe, there is no specific, or ordered human thought training, that takes place as we ALL live our lives.

Very specifically, this is with regard to the thought process that occurs in our minds on an almost moment to moment process.

Remembering, way back into my youth, a saying that was part of my growing up:

"Think, before you "act."

Yes, I was impetuous at that time of my life, things to do, life to live, what's next, and so on.

BUT NOW: so many, many, years later, now that I'm "all growed up",

I am here, referring specifically to a random thought.

Our human ability, to have a very specific, unprompted but very definitive, and very viable and authentic thought process occur, as and when we are mentally dealing with a totally different specific activity.

"A thought," and it came and was gone in a second or two.

That maybe or most probably, had absolutely, nothing to do with the subject matter, with which we were dealing, creating, or finalizing, at that time, or moment.

But, just let me go back a few paragraphs, please.

And, may we all, put our thinking caps on please?

I have mentioned elsewhere, the human thinking process is part of the way our world, our human world that is, lives its existence.

Then, as I write this, it occurs to me to wonder if our world's native animal species, have what I would call random thoughts.
The same random, intermittent thoughts, occurring as happens with ourselves.

On a personal level, I do not believe, this is possible.

I seriously believe, our earthly animal, bird, fish, kingdom species, is based on instinct, with a possible automatic knowing process of some sort.

Our human ability, to think through and resolve, to a personal satisfaction level, the answer to what might be termed a problem, or the necessity to create a possible, or realisable solution.

Thinking, as I write this, yes, another random thought, and with specific regard to our own family pets, and, just as an example;

They appear to be more motivated by actions, the actions of us their providers, for their sustenance and wellbeing.
So, maybe my previous paragraph, will or may not, be accurate, as a reality.

Sometimes, as we go about our daily activities, especially where our minds are not totally engrossed in the current job or task, that stray thought comes into existence.
I am talking here, about a thought, possibly and/or probably, is abstract, and has absolutely nothing to do with the current task.
A thought on a random subject, which has come out of absolutely nowhere.

I am also aware that as I create this chapter, my personal thought process is telling me, "I must define the application of this thought process (my thinking process) in a clear concise manner.

Surely, you might now say, "Aren't you doing this already", and my only answer might be, "isn't this just I am referring to."

Some personal thoughts, as examples:

My Great Uncle Carl, whom I have referred to elsewhere, a cabinet maker by trade and profession, used to tell me as a youngster,
"Keep your mind on the job and concentrate on the job at hand AND: hammers, chisels, and other tools; in the wrong hands can be, and are dangerous if not handled correctly."
And yet, knowing this, as I grew older and more confident in the things I get up to:
Have I, and I also include you the reader, become more complacent, or self satisfied, with time, knowledge and ability, where I/we can and do allow, our or my mind to wander, as we attend to something familiar?

Is age and experience, a reason we do not apply the same measure of concentration to the job at hand?
And, I am more than totally aware that there are other observational things I might mention at this point in time, regarding our thought processes as we grow older.

Maybe I leave these questions in abeyance now, at this point in time, as I am not qualified where psychology or psychiatric things are involved.

However, know that this chapter has somewhat rambled on about what takes place in the human mind, as we live our lives.

Thus, it could be, that there is no "one size fits all" answer to this chapter's heading.

But then, also at the same time, I still have the unanswered question in my mind, as to what takes place as we live our lives, on a daily basis, such as it is, as to, our own personal self and continued well-being.

I am now, also inclined to venture into age, as being a major factor in the random thought process developing as we grow older, and logically become older, and maybe wiser too.

I'll explain from my own memories.
As I grew up – well before the age of ten, as I have mentioned in a previous chapter. It is worth repeating.
My younger brother and I would play with dirt, toy cars, and other things like rocks and wood, in our small back yard.

I clearly remember our concentration was only on what we were doing at the time, regardless of anything else, that may have been eventuating.
Also, school became an important part of our growing up.
We were repeatedly taught to think things through, before coming up with possible answers, that may or may not be correct.
I still remember vividly an incident in early primary school when I was told repeatedly to think, before doing what I did, again.
Also, at age eight, on my mother's insistence, I started learning to play the violin, which required more aspects of thinking, and being aware of what I was doing and playing.

There was no forgiveness from mum, in playing out of tune, or, to ignore what will be thought about, and attended to.

Things like holding the instrument correctly, and playing in tune, having a regard for that which one was playing, as if you were the composer, and the possible intention behind the composing, and the piece of music.

Now, thinking back, I, and I am presuming, you too, the reader, can understand to some degree, what I will call random thinking.

It was just not allowed at all, never.
And now, in my much older age, as I learn to play something new, my mind is totally on the learning process!

That totally, maybe irrelevant thought that came or comes from seemingly nowhere.
Which, as I was learning to master the techniques of violin playing just did not, and was not mentally allowed to come into being.

Is this an important topic?
Maybe yes and yet maybe no.

Is there any importance on the random thought process that occurs in our continuing physical existence?

I believe there is, on the basis of our very individual and personal way of being alive.

Not necessarily to make us feel better, (that word better again), or to know or believe we are being true and honest to our own personal way of living.

I, personally have the belief, that, those random thoughts are, The way, and means, of helping us, to stay on track.
Whatever that track, or way of being, our personal life experience is possibly meant to be.

TO BE: that is, BE THE PERSON "WE ARE."

Success Comes From Where

It is, a very general and unspoken belief, that each and every one of us, alive and living in this human world of ours, is entitled to have a successful life.

But then, there are events and activities, as we attend to our daily work, play, adventure, and other core activity needs, that appear out of nowhere.

Events and/or things, that are sitting quietly, on that back burner, or in the background, that will need, at some time to be attended to.
But not to-day!

There are things to do, the necessaries for yourself and your family, catching up on a couple of telephone calls, making sure that this and that, which has sat undone for far too long, is attended to.
And, not forgetting the personal and/or imperative, personal, other requirements, that may need attention.

Do we create a scenario in our minds, of the day's activities, which, quite possibly, one might believe are or were, nothing more than ordinary?

Was the day, period, week, in your mind, on a very, very personal level; A SUCCESS?

And at this point in the narrative, you may possibly be, in reviewing what has just written, entitled to ask, "Success, what might it look like"?
I have achieved that which was appropriate or necessary to get things done."

So, I now ask, "Would you, or could you, look back on this day's activities, or maybe some day in the past, and know, in your mind, in some fashion, you were successful.

I might also ask; "In achieving and/or completing some things, whatever they might be, did you get to a satisfactory conclusion?"

In respect of these past lines and I have often, over the years, heard terms like, "mundane" and "soul destroying", specifically in relation to daily, but necessary tasks.

These expressions, usually refer to the believed necessary and appropriate daily activities we all find need attention.
Thus, it could be a very true, and correct affirmation.

But, and it really is a big BUT, is it possible in some way that these mundane day to day activities lead to very achievable successes?

Each and every one of us, most times, this has to be right!
AND MENTALLY, we "know" this to be right.

In respect of this comment, as an example, if something we do, goes wrong, most of us take steps, as soon as is possible to make that wrong "right."

You may say that this is fixing what went wrong.

But I now say, "You are making the wrong, right."

This sort of action is taught to us all, almost from birth.

As children, we are usually taught that life works, when you do things, and get those things right.

Just think about these last few lines for a bit.

There is no option on that one.

There are very few of us who will take criticism... ... This is just part of our being human, having to be right.

In my own vocation, that is, in my recently past professional occupation, on occasion, with a perceived difficult thought agenda, have spent considerable time and energy, taking an important item to what I believed, to be a logical conclusion.

Then, subsequently, in producing written documentation, then critically observing that which I composed, on occasion, I said to myself, what a waste of time and energy.

You did it all wrong, now start again and do it properly, THIS TIME!

On those occasions, which fortunately did not eventuate very often, the only option was to do the whole thing again.

AND, this time, get it right!

I am almost certain that this occurs to all of us, at some time or other.

Which, with this, and all the other documents making up this, shall we say, series of chapters, eventuated.

And I suspect that I am not alone in changing my thinking to have the next effort be a success.

In this instance I have avoided, purposely, the use of the word, "right". After all, this chapter is about success.

Or, for me, and I would like to think, and I trust you too, there is in life, no "right or wrong", "good or bad", "in or out", but **just** "What Is".

Thus, at those times, I am satisfied that I have achieved the desired, (or successful), outcome.

But to make that outcome into a successful conclusion is usually the last thing on my mind.
My personal thoughts are something more like, thank goodness I finished that job!" Now, what's the next thing I should attend to.

I realise this is a long, discussion about how I handle what I may term, "A successful conclusion"
And I realise, without any doubt, that this is my personal way of determining success.
AND: I know and believe, in all respects, I have had a successful life

Also, at this, and any other same time, I am also totally aware, that as individuals in this world of ours, each and every one of you reading this, can, in some way know, that without doubt, that which you undertake to completion goes way beyond right.

It is, in its own way, a success.

Maybe not a success in the eyes of other people, but a "so what".
And, add to that at the same time, a very personal thought that goes something like, "don't care".

THUS:
SUCCESS, COMES FROM YOUR OWN, VERY PERSONAL INNER SELF –

I SAY AGAIN -
YOUR INNER VERY PERSONAL SELF:

THAT PART OF YOU,
THAT YOU ALONE –
SHOULD ALWAYS ACKNOWLEDGE:

MOST IMPORTANTLY –
ALWAYS TO YOURSELF
REGARDLESS OF THE CIRCUMSTANCES

"I DID IT" – "I WAS SUCCESSFUL"! – "I AM SUCCESSFUL"!

But be careful when you "know" and "think" these words;

Total honesty and integrity, "AT ALL TIMES", must and will be your total way of "<u>BEING</u>" successful.

Volunteering

A Question:
WHAT HAPPENS WHEN YOU ARE NOT ABLE TO DO
THAT WHICH YOU VOLUNTEERED FOR? –
Each and every one of us has, at some time or in some form
or other been requested to be a volunteer.

It matters not, as regards this discussion, how the request was
made, and the circumstances that arose to make it necessary
for some person, maybe from an organization, a business, a
club, or whosoever – to make this request.

On a personal level, I am not aware of any person I have ever
known, that at some time has offered to assist in some way,
knowing well that their time is free of any charge, or cost to
another, in the act of saying yes.

It is also my belief that we offer our services, sometimes
totally unaware of exactly what we might have to do, to be
part of any team of volunteers.

Each and every one of us, offer to help others, having a regard
to our own personally known abilities, wherein we believe we
can contribute to the cause in need.

You show up on time as requested, and of course, the time
you agreed to, as well as having a rough idea of that which
you agreed to do.

SO: Back to the question -----

There are very few of us, in this world of ours, who will not offer to help if asked.
Leaving out all the various permeations of what, why, when, where, how, and the fact that most times, we really have no idea as to just what we might be getting ourselves into:

We arrive, to find that which was described, is nothing like what we see!

We arrive, to see someone, we honestly do not have any regard for, looking like they are in charge!

We arrive, to find there is no preparation, which looks like no one is in charge!

WE arrive, to discover the person running the event is someone we would not normally associate with!

We arrive, this is my turn to quickly think about fitting in somehow, and where, and how!

We do this, outside of not really, knowing where our responsibility may lie, 'cos the job description really was a little, let's say disjointed.

WELL – you are going to fit in no matter what.

Then, that which you had anticipated doing to help:
: Has been taken over by someone else
: Is no longer needed -

: Is being run by someone, a person you know, maybe, someone who should be anywhere but here.

AND, you know there is absolutely no way you are going to wriggle out of this one, and keep the peace.

AND after all, you did volunteer, possibly with good will, rather than knowledge.

Think quickly.
What to do now?

It now eventuates, that this is where the real you, comes into play!
I use the word, PLAY, very intentionally here.

In a much earlier chapter, I alluded to life; "As Being A Game".
And I stated that, at the commencement of the "game", there were no rules as the game commenced.
Common parlance uses the words, "playing a game"
As I stated there "It's a game".
And you are now involved in playing a game.

Life is a game!
The game is, to have something which is more important, than that which isn't.

Thus, one is able, that is, if the one in this instance is you, the reader: to be in a perfect place, and create a new game.

A game where you are in charge of the rules.

And the beautiful part of this game you have just created, is, that there is only "one rule":

I am in charge of what I decide to do next, and (you say to yourself) anyone can join in if they like, or don't like too, the game of that which I am doing or intend to do.

Think about this for a few moments:-
AND:
One always plays any game, with a smile on one's face.

As you finish reading this chapter, you may be wondering as to why I called this part of the book Volunteering?

It is, because as a volunteer, there are most usually no rules about what you have to do, could do, want to do, going to do!

I have used the analogy, of volunteering, as a means of demonstrating how our living life: might become.

How your life might, or may become, to a large extent, is the magic of living opportunities.

Opportunities, most of us do not take advantage of.

The game, is not to see an advantage, but create the advantage with:-

HONESTY – LOVE – INTEGRITY

AND: the JOY of the privilege of BEING - - - - - - - - - - - - - - - - - ????

It then becomes your golden opportunity to live your own life.

The life, I believe you volunteered into.

To enjoy the real you, that true person you know yourself to be.

THE ABILITY TO BE.

"WHERE THERE ARE NO RULES".

You Are The Leader

There are innumerable documents and books on leadership.

I now ask you to just up-end this book,
Now, have a good look at it's title page.

What does it say?

What does it REALLY say?

NO CHEATING PLEASE – THIS IS IMPORTANT FOR YOU!

==

"We Are – The Way"

AND – I now add:

"YOU ARE THE LEADER"

I now see you saying to yourself, something like,

"But I don't lead anyone or anything.
My job is earning a living,
It is a job, that has to be done by someone.

I am an ordinary person doing ordinary things!"

And so on.

But also, if you and I were looking for accolades because of our honesty and integrity towards others and the job we do, forget it.
IT AIN'T THERE!

BUT; each and every one of us, you and I included, are on a life's journey.

Beginning at the start of our existence on this remarkable planet we call Earth, or Mother Earth as I prefer to call it, doing just what we do.
Nothing more and nothing less.

Why are we here?
Are we achieving anything?
Are we doing the job, (whatever it may be), and,
I am alive and kicking, (as the saying goes.)

Yes, I am content to agree, that you are definitely doing the job, whatever it may be, from day to day, month to month, and year to year.

And, how do I know this, you are reading, what I am writing.

Whilst I will never know what your job is, be it work, looking after someone, staying content, creating happiness, and/or whatever else is important: -
You are alive, maybe looking to experience what's next!

In your own way! Your own very personal way:

There are those around you, those who honour you, those you look after, those who rely on you for help in times of need, those you feed, your family.

Need I go on?

You lead in an indefinable way.

A way that doesn't have to be defined.

As much as you and others would like to put a tag on a beautiful flower that has to remain, for the time being, you can remain nameless.

What we as individuals are never told is that we are "OKAY".

"You are OK, the way you are".

There is nothing to change, because, our personal way of leadership, is the way we are.

We, you and I, fail to recognise, that at this same time, we are relied on, to continually be, "The Way We Are".

Individuals all of us, with a job to do.

A job that is almost undefined, till we have completed or done that job.

As you and I are well aware, there are no rules, because each and every person living on Earth, each and every one of us, is individually driven.

We are driven by our own very personal ego, our ego that demands we be successful.

Whatever that success from time to time looks like, in our mind.

Without the necessity to explain or justify to any other person in the world, that we are, who we are, nothing more and nothing less.

Unfortunately, having regard to all legal processes, in almost all circumstances, we are called on by others, to justify, who we are, and what we do.

We are told as children, that there must be a reason why we did something.

And as adults, we carry on this tradition.

Not only with children, but to adults too, and expect a reasonable justifiable answer.

But then, as you give your own very personal response, it is mostly easier to do so, rather than create any form of angst for others.
Move on, with your own personal ego totally intact and without unnecessary argument.

As I compose these last few sentences, I am very personally aware that I more than tend not to compromise my own methods of life and living.
I personally decided, a long, long time ago, that I am, who I am.
As a Justice Of The Peace, when any people come to me for assistance in the validation of documents, invariably as they approach me, there is an attempt at an explanation for the reason they wish my assistance.

I always interrupt, politely of course, to let them know I am there to assist them, and please, I don't need to know why. I love the smiles I get at that time, when, something can be done without justification.

You may be wondering why I am going down this particular path?

I truly believe that leadership is about knowing without question, an absolute belief in yourself, warts and all.

Previously. I touched on the fact that, "We are OKAY, AS WE ARE", or "THE WAY WE ARE", and this I believe is, and should always be your form of leadership.

JUST BE GAME ENOUGH!

Rejoice in truly knowing yourself as the person you are, that individual, the person who is working their way through life and living.

Interestingly, I sense you saying to yourself, something like; But, I don't lead anyone or anything, that has to be done, I do the job that has to be done.
I am an ordinary person, and do ordinary things, that have to be done.
And, so on!

But also, IF, you and I are looking for accolades because of our honesty and integrity towards all others, and the job we do, forget it.
IT AIN'T THERE! – as I said before.

For life, has its personal ups and downs, whatever they might be.

Love the personal challenges, accolades, victories and whatever else comes along.

THIS IS LIFE!

THIS IS BEING ALIVE!

THIS IS LIVING!

Growing Older

As we progress through the years, what might growing older mean to you, the reader, of this chapter?

Always remember, it is important! – Age is only a number.
To-day you are older than yesterday.
And, believe it or not, younger than tomorrow.

As I compose this chapter, I might be referring to a person just reaching their teenage years, or someone who is just about to gain the privilege of voting, or perhaps someone who is considering marriage, or even you the reader.
Who knows?
I have reason to believe, maybe because of my age, that as we age, we mature somewhat into a position of acceptance of our environment.

The environment very well might be regarded as the circumstances created through those years we have lived.

But, I am staying clear, of any circumstances that may have created your lifestyle or environment as you currently live in it, or have lived in it in past years.

This chapter is to be more about how we see ourselves, say, this year, as against past years.

As I Look back on my life, some memories are very clear, some memories are somewhat forgotten, and some memories have gone forever.

A personal example. Something I have mentioned before somewhere, and it deserves repeating.

As a boy of 15, I joined the Royal Australian Navy as a musician. I had learnt the violin from the age of seven, but you will realize this is not an instrument to play on parade, so I was given an alto saxophone to learn to play, and ultimately became a reasonably proficient clarinet player.

It is immaterial, at this point, as to how a Saxophone became a Clarinet.

Moving on a few years, with navy experiences and ranking increments, I became an instructor (for some time) in the Australian Navy School of Music.

Recently at a reunion of ex-navy musicians, I was approached by someone I did not remember – someone who remembered me – with expressions of thanks for the time I spent with him teaching him to play an instrument, and thereby assisting him to become a competent musician.

Incidentally, the instrument was a Bassoon, and as there was no other available woodwind instructor, I got the job.

Sure, he was one of many I taught in those years, and it might be acceptable to forget a particular individual.

But why, had my attention given him in that learning period of his, totally disappeared from my memories? And even now, a few years later, I do not remember his name but, funnily enough remember his stature – he had a stature as being someone, with a great personal presence.

I did however remember, as he mentioned the Bassoon, the conversation about me not being a bassoon player, but it was my job to teach him, and we got on with his learning experiences.

At the same time, I can still vividly recall some very early boyhood memories and also of my earlier childhood.

As partially mentioned elsewhere; playing, with my younger brother, in the back yard, under the lemon tree in the dirt, or the wooden steps down to be back yard, under which grew the most magnificent forms of moss, lichen and ferns, to wonder about.
Then at the same time, there is another memory.

As a member of the Navy Band I was part of the opening ceremony at the 1956 Melbourne Olympics. I will not forget the memory of the band – 100 strong – forming the five Olympic circles; I was next behind one of the two Bass Drums. But, most memorable was the huge roar of approval from the crowd (100,000 plus) when the drum majors ignited smoke flares, coming from the tops of their maces while we marched in circle formation.

I believe that each and every one of you reading this will be the same as I.
Vivid memories of some things and total forgetfulness of something else.

This now brings me to a request.

Would it be appropriate for you to take some time out, and review life memories?

Would it assist you in some undefinable way, to record in writing, (maybe using an IPad or computer) things you remember.

As I compose the previous sentence, I am also totally aware that there probably,
or will be occasions and events that you decided were never to be mentioned again.

As we grow older, our life experiences impinge on our current view of life as we have experienced it over the years.

Some of you will be able to look back over your memories and be content with what you remember.

Some of you will not be content to do the same thing. Your memories of some things, could be too raw for you to recall.

I do believe implicitly that each of us is the creation of the environments in which we grew up, aged and became older.

You are – just who you are.

Have no regrets that you are that person.

There is no way that you can alter the past and the creation of who you are now.

BUT – what of the future?

The future for each of us is our growing older
Be it a day to day situation, with excitement about a planned event or activity, or just knowing life is as it is, and let's get on with it.

You will realize it is not possible for me to cover the many permutations that may make up your personality, the one that you know so well.

Nor do I wish to impose on you the aspect of how I might regard my ability to grow older.

This chapter I regard as a given, to be a part of the overall concept of "The Way-We Are".

Be content that you are who you are!

You, or others, may wish to be someone other than that real you.

It matters not to any other person in this world of ours, what age you are at this point in time.

Memoirs, in a written form could be of importance to family members, no matter how many years hence that might be.

And as I make this comment, I realise I personally have no intention of putting any part of my life story into writing.
Except that, in small pieces, if they come into contact with this writing... ... ...
And yet, on re-reading previous chapters and also what may yet be written, is a story, partly of my life and how I have lived it.

We all have cherished memories.
We all have things we've forgotten.
We all have things we determined will never be mentioned again.

But, maybe!

Printed in the United States
By Bookmasters